Graham Saunders

Patrick Marber's
Closer

continuum

Continuum

The Tower Building, 11 York Road, London SE1 7NX

80 Maiden Lane, Suite 704, New York NY 10038

www.continuumbooks.com

First published 2008

British Library Cataloguing-in-Publication Data
A catalogue record for this book is available from the British Library.

ISBN: 978-0-8264-9205-0 (hardback)
           978-0-8264-9248-7 (paperback)

Library of Congress Cataloging-in-Publication Data
A catalog record for this book is available from the Library of Congress.

Typeset by Kenneth Burnley, Wirral, Cheshire
Printed and bound in Great Britain by MPG Books Ltd, Bodmin, Cornwall

Patrick Marber's
Closer

Continuum Modern Theatre Guides

Arthur Miller's Death of a Salesman
Peter L. Hays and Kent Nicholson

August Wilson's Fences
Ladrica Menson-Furr

Caryl Churchill's Top Girls
Alicia Tycer

David Mamet's Oleanna
David Sauer

John Osborne's Look Back in Anger
Aleks Sierz

Samuel Beckett's Waiting for Godot
Mark Taylor-Batty and Juliette Taylor-Batty

Sarah Kane's Blasted
Helen Iball

Tom Stoppard's Arcadia
John Fleming

Tony Kushner's Angels in America
Ken Nielsen

Contents

General Preface

Continuum Modern Theatre Guides

Volumes in the series Continuum Modern Theatre Guides offer concise and informed introductions to the key plays of modern times. Each book takes a close look at one particular play's dramaturgical qualities and then at its various theatrical manifestations. The books are carefully structured to offer a systematic study of the play in its biographical, historical, social and political context, followed by an in-depth study of the text and a chapter which outlines the work's production history, examining both the original productions of the play and subsequent major stage interpretations. Where relevant, screen adaptations will also be analysed. There then follows a chapter dedicated to workshopping the play, based on suggested group exercises. Also included are a timeline and suggestions for further reading.

Each book covers:

- Background and context
- Analysis of the play
- Production history
- Workshopping exercises

The aim is to provide accessible introductions to modern plays for students in both Theatre/Performance Studies and English, as well as for informed general readers. The series includes up-to-date coverage of a broad range of key plays, with summaries of important critical approaches and the intellectual debates that have illuminated the meaning of the work and made a significant contribution to our broader cultural life. They will enable readers to develop their understanding of playwrights and theatre-makers, as well as inspiring them to broaden their studies.

The Editors:
Steve Barfield, Janelle Reinelt,
Graham Saunders and Aleks Sierz

March 2008

Acknowledgements

I would like to thank my fellow series editors, who have offered intellectual, practical and moral support throughout: Steve Barfield, Janelle Reinelt and Aleks Sierz. The same also applies to Anna Sandeman, Rebecca Simmonds and Colleen Coalter at Continuum.

Much of the material in Chapter 4, 'Workshopping the Play', came out of practical sessions with my students at the University of Reading. I would like to thank them all collectively for their enthusiasm, input and interrogation of the exercises. The following colleagues also offered advice and information on their own practical engagement in teaching *Closer*: Gilli Bush-Bailey (Royal Holloway), Selina Busby (Central School of Speech & Drama), Anthony Frost (UEA), Dan Rebellato (Royal Holloway), Tim Moss (Huddersfield), David Pattie (Chester), Stuart Hampton-Reeves (University of Central Lancashire), George Rodosthenous (Leeds), Lib Taylor (Reading) and Mark Westbrook (Ulster).

Amanda Bull's patience and good humour have also been much appreciated.

Permission to quote from Patrick Marber: *Plays 1* are reproduced by permission from Methuen Publishing Ltd.

A note on the text
All quotations from *Closer*, unless otherwise specified come from *Plays: 1*, London: Methuen, 1997.

Graham Saunders
Bristol

1 Background and Context

Introduction

This chapter is an introduction to the study of Patrick Marber's *Closer*. It explains why the play is important, gives a sketch of its author's life and discusses the social, economic and political background to the play.

Since its first production in 1997, Patrick Marber's *Closer* has become recognized as one of the most significant British plays of the 1990s. It is also an example of a work that marked the resurgence of provocative and ground-breaking new theatre writing in Britain during this decade. Plays such as Phyllis Nagy's *The Strip* (1995), Sarah Kane's *Blasted* (1995) and Mark Ravenhill's *Shopping and Fucking* (1996) not only made important innovations in theatrical form, but also made loud noises in drawing people's attention to the theatre itself – a medium often considered at best conservative or at worst moribund in terms of its cultural relevance. However, *Closer* is distinguishable from many of its contemporaries in a number of ways: while in *simpatico* with much new writing of the late 1990s by being darkly savage in theme and mood, *Closer* was also a popular success with both West End and Broadway audiences.

Closer has also been translated and performed in over thirty countries worldwide, while in Britain – with the notable exception of Sarah Kane's work – it was one of the first examples of a play from the 1990s being revived in the new millennium. In early 2001 *Closer* was performed on the main stage of the Birmingham

Repertory Theatre: such revivals provide strong indications that a new play has somehow 'passed the test' and has joined an established canon/repertoire of popular/frequently performed work.

Closer not only enjoyed considerable favour from theatre critics at the time, but also quickly merited academic attention with significant entries within major surveys of twentieth-century British playwriting. These include Christopher Innes' revised volume, *Modern British Drama* in 2002 and David Rabey's *English Drama since 1940* in 2003.

Closer is also notable for being made into a film and, while several British plays from this period also underwent adaptation including Jez Butterworth's *Mojo* (1995; film 1997), Judy Upton's *Ashes and Sand* (1994; film 2002) and Michael Frayn's *Copenhagen* (1998; film 2002), in the main these film versions were produced by small British companies, and also largely confined to an indigenous market. In contrast, *Closer,* with its high profile director and cast, including Julia Roberts and Natalie Portman, was released worldwide as a major Hollywood film in 2004.

Much of *Closer*'s success comes from its intense scrutiny of human behaviour and sexuality. The critic Aleks Sierz believes that it was 'arguably the decade's key play about relationships, and certainly one of the most successful' (Sierz 2001: 187), while Sir Richard Eyre, (who as Artistic Director of the Royal National Theatre had commissioned Marber's play), goes further by drawing attention to *Closer* being one of a handful of British plays – others include Shakespeare's *Twelfth Night* (c.1601), John Osborne's *Look Back in Anger* (1956) and Tom Stoppard's *The Real Thing* (1982) – which treat the theme of sex frankly and unsparingly.

Closer is also unusual in being one of the few plays of the 1990s that was both self-consciously modern and metropolitan in its sensibility – the critic Christopher Innes for instance calls it 'aggressively contemporary' (Innes 2002: 433) – yet it also employs a dramatic structure based around the somewhat unfashionable term of the 'well-made play'. So while in 2001 the critic Aleks Sierz made Marber a central figure in his book *In-Yer-Face Theatre: British Drama Today* about the provocative young playwrights who defined much of the new theatre writing during the 1990s, *Closer*'s uncompromising subject matter was organized within a dramatic structure often associated with a number of older playwrights including Noel Coward and Terence Rattigan, who were writing much of their best known work during the 1930s and 1940s. These contradictory forces made *Closer* something of a theatrical oddity among the rash of so-called 'in-yer-face' plays during the mid-/late 1990s, which were notable for the degree of explicitness through which they depicted violent and sexual acts.

About Patrick Marber

Patrick Marber was born in London on 19 September 1964 and grew up in Wimbledon, London. He was schooled at Rokeby Preparatory School, Kingston-upon-Thames, then St Paul's School London and Cranleigh School, Surrey before going to Wadham College, Oxford University where he read English. After leaving university Marber worked for five years as a stand-up comedian touring throughout England.

However, Marber's real breakthrough came in 1992 when he began co-writing and sometimes appearing as a performer in some of the most popular and innovative comedy programmes for radio and television during the early to mid-1990s. The critic Peter Buse comments that 'these highly self-referential shows fiercely parodied televisual genres (broadcast news, talk shows, video diaries) in some of the most scabrous comedy of recent years' (Buse 2006), and included shows such as *On the Hour* (BBC Radio 4, 1992) and *The Day Today* (BBC2, 1994), which gave rise to Steve Coogan's memorable comic creation Alan Partridge. Marber also co-wrote and appeared in the spin-off wireless and television series which featured Partridge/Coogan, *Knowing me Knowing You* (BBC Radio 4 and BBC2, 1994–5). Marber has said that these years as a performer/writer prepared him for writing and directing both his own plays and the work of others: 'It gave me an ear for an audience, an ear for a certain kind of rhythm of speech' (Pride 2004).

With such a body of popular and critically acclaimed work, the most likely course would have been for Marber to continue working in wireless and television as a comedy scriptwriter. However, in February 1995 he produced his first full length play, *Dealer's Choice*, although Christopher Innes points out that this apparent shift in working medium was not so surprising when one took into account several other stand-up comedians/writers of the 1990s – most notably Ben Elton – who had also made similar forays into the theatre in order 'to depict their social criticism in comic terms' (Innes 2002: 427).

Dealer's Choice is also unusual in that it did not follow the normal route of being a fully realized script; rather it went through a process Marber has described as 'rehearsed readings, improvisations and a small scale production' (Marber 2004: xv). These took place between November 1993 and December 1994 at the National Theatre Studio, with the actual production itself taking place on its Cottesloe stage in February 1995. Marber also took the unusual step for a first time playwright by directing the production himself. This first major foray into theatre was both a critical and a commercial success. *Dealer's Choice* transferred to the West End Vaudeville Theatre in May where it ran until October; it also won the Evening Standard Award for Best Comedy and the Writer's Guild award for Best West End Play in the same year before going on an international tour in 1996.

Marber's next project in 1995 also went against received expectations, when he returned back to television, this time as adapter for a classic drama. As part of BBC2's *Performance* series, in which canonical plays were adapted for television Marber was approached to write a version of August Strindberg's *Miss Julie* (1888), which shows a brutal struggle of class and gender between the aristocratic Miss Julie of the title and her servant Jean. Again, Marber directed the production himself, but rather than faithfully rendering Strindberg's play he set out to make some significant changes: called *After Miss Julie* (1995), Marber has commented, 'The play is not a translation of the original. Rather it is a "version" – with all the ambiguity that word might suggest. I was unfaithful to the original. But conscious that infidelity might be an act of love' (Marber 2004: xv). While broadly recognizable in terms of its characters and events, *After Miss Julie* was notable for relocating the play to Britain on the 26 July 1945, the eve of the post-war Labour Party victory.

After Miss Julie marks an important juncture in Marber's work, as many of the themes and ideas of *Closer* are prefigured in Strindberg's play. He has commented that, 'I suspect my work on *Miss Julie* had got me thinking about this sort of territory' (Marber 2004: xvi). These shared concerns include the powerful attraction of sexual desire, but also the pessimistic depiction of relationships between men and women being essentially antagonistic – struggles for power that are often played out as a battles to the death.

Marber later adapted the television play for stage version which was performed in 2003 at the Donmar Warehouse, directed by Michael Grandage.

Based on the success of *Dealer's Choice*, Richard Eyre commissioned another play from Marber. The play, which was completed at the end of 1996 was to be *Closer*, and again it confounded expectations. *Dealer's Choice,* with its all male cast and a plot based around a poker game seemed to follow a spate of plays that had come out that year: these included Simon Block's *Not a Game for Boys*, Jez Butterworth's *Mojo* and William Gaminara's *According to Hoyle*. In these plays masculine bonds constitute the principal subject matter, but their focus on masculine identity was often narrowly defined, and dissipated through an appropriation of comic form. Taking his title from the second album of the introspective beat group Joy Division, *Closer* was to be a very different play in every respect.

Closer premiered at the 300-seat Cottesloe Auditorium in May 1997, again directed by Marber. The Cottesloe is the smallest theatre space at the Royal National Theatre and traditionally the place where new work receives its premiere. The play was a success and by October it had moved to the larger 890-seat Lyttleton Theatre; by the following year it had transferred to the West End, opening at the Lyric Theatre in March 1998, where it ran until October. This was followed by a successful Broadway run (again with Marber directing the production) from March to September 1999.

Seven years after its stage debut, *Closer* underwent a further metamorphosis, this time as a screen version in 2004. Its director Mike Nichols had seen the play in London, and met Marber during Spring 1999 while the production was on Broadway to discuss the viability of a film adaptation. Although reluctant at first, after the New York production had finished Marber felt ready to re-evaluate the merits of adapting *Closer* for a new medium.

Marber's next major play *Howard Katz* in 2001, again premiered at the Royal National Theatre and was directed by the playwright. Although received favourably in some quarters, the play did not quite enjoy the critical and commercial success of *Dealer's Choice* or *Closer*, perhaps because, as Peter Buse comments, 'the play's unfashionable interest in judgement and redemption . . . made *Howard Katz* difficult for contemporary London audiences to digest' (Buse 2006).

Since *Howard Katz*, Marber has written relatively little for theatre, although in the same year he was one among many well known dramatists who collaborated in a project called *The Chain Play* for a one off performance at the Royal National Theatre. In 2004 Marber also wrote a play called *The Musicians*, as part of the

Shell Connections project, as a specially commissioned play for young people. Marber has also written two short television films (*The Egg* in 2002 and *Old Street* in 2004) and a radio play (*Hoop Lane*, Radio 3, 2004) in the intervening period. However, in November 2006 he made a high profile return to the theatre with *Don Juan in Soho*, a free adaptation much in the tradition of *After Miss Julie* of Molière's *Don Juan* (1665).

Marber's energies in recent years have also been taken up with adapting novels for film versions. These have included Patrick McGrath's *Asylum*, which was released in 2004, and Zoë Heller's *Notes on a Scandal,* which his former mentor Sir Richard Eyre directed in 2007.

Marber is also a noted director of other people's work and his productions include Dennis Potter's *Blue Remembered Hills* (National, 1996), Craig Raine's *1953* (Almedia, 1996), David Mamet's *The Old Neighborhood* (Royal Court, 1998) and Harold Pinter's *The Caretaker* (Comedy Theatre, 2000). In 1999 Marber also made his professional stage debut in a 2000 West End production of David Mamet's *Speed the Plow*, which he followed up in 2002 at the Royal National Theatre in a show entitled *Sketches*, comprised of a series of short works by Harold Pinter. Marber appeared in a piece entitled *Trouble in the Works*.

The social and cultural context

In the latest published version of *Closer* Patrick Marber makes a small but significant cut to the opening scene. While retaining its principal London setting, he removed a note included in previous editions, which makes specific reference to the play being set in the 1990s. Presumably Marber wanted to make *Closer* more 'universal' in scope, yet several critics, including Christopher Innes, saw the play as an archetypal metropolitan 1990s drama, commenting that 'the way the characters are depicted as almost hermetically sealed

off from the world around them is an image of isolation and disso-
ciation that epitomizes the self-absorbed "Me" generation of the
1990s' (Innes 2002: 431); even the film version, released in 2004,
was still considered by one critic to be 'frozen in 1997' (Sandhu
2005: 21). In some respects this specificity is unavoidable, since no
work can ever distance itself completely from the time and culture
that surrounds it, and *Closer* is forged out of certain ideas and
debates that were current in British society during the 1990s.

On the most obvious level was the play's topical exploration of
new technology. In its most celebrated scene, theatre-goers in 1997
perhaps for the first time witnessed an onstage representation of
two people communicating through the internet. Although the
World Wide Web had been increasingly taken up by non-
computer specialists since 1993, it was still something of a novelty
for many. The same went for mobile phones which also made one
of their first appearances in *Closer*. That the representation of this
technology was so new at the time is demonstrated in the 1999
edition of the play when Larry, after being asked by Dan whether
he frequently visits the online environment, is simply confused,
and Dan has to specify 'Net' (Marber 1999: 21). However, by the
time of the 2004 edition such was the ubiquity of the internet that
Marber could now safely delete such explanatory pointers. Yet, by
the same token, the introduction of new technical innovations also
risks dating the play. For instance, when Alice borrows Dan's
mobile telephone, the text reads, 'she pulls out the aerial with her
teeth' (Marber 1999: 10); needless to say, this stage direction was
cut by the 2004 edition.

The premiere of *Closer* in May 1997 took place during the same
month in which the Labour Party under Tony Blair won a landslide
election victory. Since 1979 Britain had been governed by the Conservative administrations of Margaret Thatcher and John Major,
and it was felt that with the election of the first Labour government
since 1974 widespread political and social change would be initi-

ated by the Blair government.

Prior to the election, 'New Labour' (as the party had rebranded itself) had closely associated itself with high profile events that had been taking place in various branches of the arts. Dubbed 'Cool Britannia', this brief cultural period reached its zenith in 1997, where beat groups such as Blur and Oasis, conceptual artists such as Damien Hirst and Tracey Emin and indeed dramatists such as Patrick Marber were seen to have engendered a youthfully vigorous and creative Britain. While the critic Vera Gottlieb argued that the term was essentially a construction of media and public relation companies (Gottlieb and Chambers 1999: 209), fellow critic Ken Urban argues, 'The art felt new because of the young fashionable people making it' (Urban 2004: 358).

In some aspects *Closer* was the archetypal play that represented many of the characteristics associated with the term 'Cool Britannia'. These ranged from its contemporary metropolitan setting, its self-conscious 'coolness', its underlying preoccupation with the surface appearance of things and an accompanying cynicism and bleakness as audiences witnessed the machinations of its characters. Yet like so much of the play itself, judging *Closer* by its surface alone could prove deceptive.

Patrick Marber has commented that the writing of *Closer* came about due to his awareness that a particular juncture had been reached in the mid 1990s, whereby 'after feminist politics and the age of the New Man . . . no one knows what's going on anymore' (Sierz 2001: 191). This alludes to both the state of indeterminacy governing the conduct of heterosexual relationships in western society, and the challenges and reassessment to feminist thinking that had came from a number of quarters during the 1990s. Some might argue 'reassessment' is the wrong term to use, and that the title of Susan Faludi's influential book *Backlash: The Undeclared War Against Women* (1992) was perhaps a more accurate term to describe the challenges to feminist practice in the 1990s. Feminism as both a term and ideal came under direct attack in books such as David Thomas's *Not Guilty* (1993), which variously blamed feminism for the breakdown of society since the 1960s and a corresponding marginalization of men's roles; also women such as Naomi Wolf's *Fire with Fire: The New Female Power and how it will change the 21st Century* (1993), openly criticized aspects of feminist theory and activism that had gone before. This indeterminate state in which feminism entered the 1990s left something of an ideological vacuum, a symptom of which was reflected in the nebulous term 'Post-Feminism'.

Allied to this, and indeed perhaps as a direct result of the attention feminism had already paid to analysing patriarchal structures in society, attention now turned to questions and definitions of masculinity. Put crudely and simplistically, if the 1980s was the decade when notions of femininity occupied a prominent place in mainstream culture, then the 1990s was the decade when representations of masculinity promulgated themselves in popular culture and the arts.

The playwright David Edgar has commented that in British theatre at least, a number of male-centred plays in the 1990s, including Nick Grosso's *Peaches* (1994) and Marber's *Dealer's Choice*, 'address masculinity and its discontents as demonstrably as the plays of the early 1960's [*sic*] addressed class and those of the 1970's [*sic*] the failures of democracy . . . The decline of the dominant role of men – in the workplace and in the family – is probably the biggest single story of the last thirty years in the western countries (Edgar 1999: 27–8).

Edgar's observation about new writing in theatre was reflected by a corresponding trend in novels such as Nick Hornby's *High Fidelity* (1995), Blake Morrison's *And when did you last see your father* (1993) and Tony Parsons' *Man and Boy* (2000); it could also be seen in films such as *The Full Monty* (1997) and *Billy Elliot* (2000).

However, while these and plays such as Joe Penhall's *Pale Horse* (1994) or David Eldridge's *Serving it up* (1996) are thoughtful, if violent explorations of male identity, other plays and especially films from the period actively appeared to not only celebrate a world dominated by violent and reckless forms of masculinity, but one in which women were notably absent or simply used as vehicles for abuse. These included films such as Quentin Tarantino's *Reservoir Dogs* (1992), Neil La Butes' *In the Company of Men* (1997) and Guy Ritchie's *Lock Stock and Two Smoking Barrels* (1998).

While British theatre during this period saw plays such as Jonathan Harvey's *Beautiful Thing* (1993) and Kevin Elyot's *My Night with Reg* (1994), which explored aspects of masculine homosexual identity, often in a thoughtful and humorous way, like its counterparts in film many other plays focused on wild sprees of violent behaviour; rather than being 'in crisis', plays such as Anthony Neilson's *Penetrator* (1994), Tracey Letts' *Killer Joe* (1995) and Louis Mellis and David Scinto's *Gangster No. 1* (1995) often seemed to advocate a violent masculinity.

This celebration of the irresponsible male also manifested itself, albeit less violently, throughout British popular culture during the mid-/late 1990s. This ranged from the launch of the men's magazine *Loaded* in 1994, to television series such as *Fantasy Football League* (1994–6) and *The Word* (1990–5), which all embraced 'traditional' male pursuits such as drinking, football and ogling (via the non-threatening distance provided by the barriers of page and television screen) scantily clad women.

The media quickly found a term for this form of masculinity – 'The New Lad'. Often university educated and from the professional classes – the 'New Lad' – while familiar with the concept of feminism, and broadly in agreement with its aims, still celebrated an unashamed form of 'male' behaviour. James Brown, the editor of *Loaded,* provided a rationale of sorts:

We like football, but that doesn't mean we're hooligans. We like drinking but it doesn't mean that as a soon as the pub shuts we turn into wife beating misogynists. We like looking at pictures of fancy ladies sometimes, but that doesn't mean we want to rape them (Southwell 1998: 101)

The critic Imelda Whelehan provides an alternative view to this composite of the New Lad in the following terms: 'Self-centred, male identified, leering and obsessed by sport, the new lad was naughty but nice; he proved himself a domestic catastrophe, but a certain boylike vulnerability supposedly made up for his deficiencies' (Whelehan 2000: 5).

Like the nostalgic feel associated with Cool Britannia's 'Brit-pop', in which 'new' bands such as Blur and Oasis looked back to a lost English sensibility via a homage to 1960s' groups such as The Beatles and The Kinks, Whelean observes that allied to the bravado of the New Lad was an accompanying melancholia 'for a lost, uncomplicated past populated by "real" women and humorous cheeky chappies' (Whelehan 2000: 11). Its heroes were drawn from the *Carry On* series of films from the 1960s and 1970s, where ageing roué's such as Sid James and Leslie Philips could indulge in prurient lechery: it was a prelapsarian age without risk of censure.

However, Whelehan argues that the beneath the seaside postcard nostalgia the figure of the New Lad was symptomatic of a gender conflict that had been identified since the end of the 1990s in books such as Joan Smith's *Misogynies* (1989) and the aforementioned *Backlash* by Susan Faludi. In short, a counter-insurgency had been launched against the gains made by feminism, and that the rise to prominence of the New Lad was symptomatic of an attempt to undermine and wrest power from women:

From a feminist position it is difficult not to interpret the new lad as a nostalgic revival of old patriarchy; a direct challenge to feminism's call for social transformation by reaffirming – albeit 'ironically' – the unchanging nature of gender relations and sexual roles. (Whelehan 2000: 6)

Some sort of 'equality' came in the form of a counterpart – or perhaps accessory – to the 'New Lad': the so-called 'Ladette'. In some respects this startling figure was not entirely new, and was reminiscent to the unruly 'Roaring Girls' of Jacobean drama. In the 1990s its most high profile representation came through the brief, but immensely successful career of The Spice Girls. Their film *Spice World: The Movie* was released the same year as *Closer*, and though ostensibly an all female pop group, The Spice Girls associated themselves with a loose but all governing ideology called 'Girl Power'. Elaine Aston succinctly assesses this as 'a contradictory mix of feminist and anti-feminist discourses that promoted an image of aggressive "sisterhood" and feminine glamour through a creed of selfish individualism designed to "get what you want out of life"' (Aston 2003: 6).

The Ladette was meant to take on the 'New Lad' at their own game, and television programmes such as *The Girlie Show* (1995), showed young women competing with their male counterparts through drinking and lecherous banter. The critics John McRae and Ronald Carter argue that the Ladette even gave rise to a new sub-genre in the novel known as 'Chick Lit' (McRae and Carter 2004: 31); this is perhaps best exemplified by the phenomenal success of Helen Fielding's eponymous heroine from the novel (and subsequent film) *Bridget Jones's Diary* (1996).

Yet while this figure seemed to capture the public imagination, its *modus operandi* was predicated on modes of behaviour set down and prescribed by men. Like Elaine Aston, Imelda Whelehan argues that adopting patriarchal behaviour 'offers the most shallow model of gender equality [as it] suggests that women could or should adopt the most anti-social and pointless of "male" behaviour as a sign of empowerment (Whelehan 2000: 6). Signs of the strains that 'keeping up' and readily accepting the terms dictated by men can be seen in the more reflective passages of Fielding's novel, where Bridget is at times left feeling vulnerable with her own undefined and confused self-image as a woman.

Patrick Marber's comment about *Closer* being inspired through the gender confusions thrown up by terms such as 'post-feminism' and 'new man' at least offered some alternative to the terms New Lad/Ladette, although eventually it would prove just as unsatisfactory for all concerned. William Gaminara, whose play *According to Hoyle* written in the same year as *Dealer's Choice* (and another all male play about a group of poker players), commented that the term New Man was 'very much a media concept from the start, targeted very particularly at the middle classes, but which nevertheless a lot of men took on board as something that they might want, and that women might want as well'. However, Gaminara concludes that ultimately men's engagement with the concept rarely extended any further than 'yet another in a long line of newfangled techniques to get women into bed' (Edgar 1999: 54).

This indeterminate state of affairs in the mid- to late 1990s could be glimpsed in British theatre by a series of plays which seemed to respond to this confusion by not only polarizing representations of gender, but set them – and at times violently – in direct opposition to one another. Significant examples included Sarah Kane's *Blasted, Phaedra's Love* (1996), *Cleansed* (1998) and Anthony Neilson's *The Censor* (1997). Fellow playwright Mark Ravenhill makes a link to the representations of violent masculinity in these plays coming out of a perceived crisis in heterosexual relations during the 1990s:

So deep are the suspicions and tensions between heterosexual men and women that it is almost impossible to stage their relationships. The male and female parts of our psyches are pushing further and further apart and to bring them together on stage can only result in a huge conflict. (Edgar 1999: 50)

While plays such as David Hare's *Skylight* (1995) and Marber's *Closer* do not look at gender relations through such extreme contrasts, the 'suspicions and tensions' that Ravenhill observes are evident in both. While Marber has commented that the writing of *Closer* came about because, 'I just thought that there wasn't a play addressing the romantic concerns of my particular generation at that particular time' (Motskin 2004: 34), the fractious nature of pre-millennial relationships also dominates the play.

2 Analysis and Commentary

Plot Summary

This chapter is a study of *Closer* both as a dramatic text and as a performed play that has excited comment and provoked analysis. Although plot summaries are often seen as old-fashioned, they are useful in sketching out the action of the play, before undertaking a broader analysis of its characters, influences, images, themes and key scenes.

Closer is set in London and over the duration of its twelve scenes follows four adults – Dan, Alice, Larry and Anna – over the course of a four-and-a-half-year period as they come together, break apart, swap partners and eventually separate irrevocably.

The play opens at a hospital where Daniel Woolf, a newspaper obituary writer, has brought a young girl Alice Ayres, who he witnessed in a taxi accident. Alice, who defines herself with the enigmatic phrase, 'I'm a waif' (1:1.191) has arrived in London the previous day from New York where she has been working as a stripper. Their conversation starts out as a flirtatious and witty battle of repartee, but soon changes to a form of courtship. We are also briefly introduced to Larry, a dermatologist who cursorily examines and becomes interested in the aetiology of a scar on Alice's leg, which she explains was caused by a truck in America.

Scene two takes place 15 months later, in which time Dan and Alice have become lovers. Dan has given up his job and has written a novel loosely based on his relationship with Alice. The scene opens at Anna's photographic studio where he is having his picture taken for the forthcoming novel which Anna has enthusiastically read; however, she dislikes the title and suggests a new one: 'The Aquarium' (1:2.197). She explains that she often goes to the Aquarium at London Zoo to photograph strangers as part of an exhibition she is planning.

Dan is immediately attracted to Anna and kisses her. Anna is separated from her husband, and although evident that she is also attracted to Dan, points out, 'I don't want trouble' and 'You're taken' (1:2.200). Alice arrives, and while she is in the lavatory Dan insists that he must see Anna again. Alice returns and asks if Anna will also take her photograph. When they are alone Alice tells Anna that she overhead her conversation with Dan. Anna takes Alice's picture and tries to reassure her by saying, 'I'm not a thief' (1:2.203).

Scene three takes place in two different locations. Dan is at home in his flat and Larry, the doctor from scene one, is in his office. However, both are communicating to each other via an internet sex chat room. Dan adopts the female persona of 'Anna' and the scene ends with Larry arranging to meet the following day at the Aquarium in London Zoo.

Scene four shows the meeting between Larry and the real Anna, who happens to be at the Aquarium on her birthday. A comic scene of misunderstanding ensues, until Anna realizes that Dan is the likely prankster, although Larry finds it hard to believe that a man could so convincingly masquerade as a woman.

Scene five takes place five months afterwards at the launch of Anna's photographic exhibition. In the interim we learn that Anna and Larry have started a relationship one month after their first meeting at the Aquarium. The portrait of Alice that Anna took in scene two is one of the exhibits, and both Alice and Dan are attending the opening. Dan's book has been a critical and commercial failure and he is considering going back to his old job as a newspaper obituarist. Forebodings of the encounter between Anna and

Alice in scene two re-emerge with Alice saying that she is waiting for Dan to leave her (1:5.214). Alice also wants to come to the funeral of Dan's father that weekend, but he wishes to attend the event alone immediately after the exhibition.

Larry and Alice meet again. On learning that Larry is Anna's boyfriend Alice flirts with him. He notices again the scar on Alice's leg, which on this occasion she explains came about from a car crash in which both her parents died. Despite not seeing her for a year we learn that Dan has been silently pursuing Anna; he is scathing about Larry and pleads with Anna to come away that weekend to his father's funeral.

Scene six takes place one year later. Described by Marber as 'verbally the most brutal moment' (Raab 2002: 144), parallel scenes reveal Anna and Dan preparing to leave their respective partners. The scene between Dan and Alice is much shorter, but no less brutal than the painfully wrought confrontation between Larry and Anna.

We learn that in the intervening year Anna and Larry have married. Larry has returned home after a medical conference in New York and confesses that during the trip he slept with a prostitute. Anna also confesses that she has been having an affair with Dan since the night of her exhibition. Larry's response to her betrayal is to demand details of their most intimate sexual infidelities.

Act two takes place six months after the respective break-ups. Larry is in the private room of a lap dancing club with Alice, who maintains an elaborate charade of pretending not to know of either him or Dan. Larry's desire to know the full sexual details of Anna's infidelity takes another form in this scene where he becomes obsessed with Alice revealing her real name. When she tells him her real name is Jane Jones, Larry does not believe her and even pays five hundred and sixty pounds for the answer. 'Alice's' reply is the same: 'My real name is Plain-Jane-Jones' (2:7.246). The scene ends with Larry making Alice strip for him.

Scene eight takes place one month afterwards at a restaurant. Dan has arranged to meet Anna in order to find out whether Larry has agreed to sign divorce papers. The scene moves back to their lunchtime meeting at the same restaurant, where Larry offers to sign the divorce papers under one condition: that they go back to his surgery for 'our final fuck . . . Be my whore and in return I will pay you with your liberty' (2:8.254). Anna reluctantly assents to Larry's demand, but her guilt is detected by Dan who comments, 'It's gone . . . we're not innocent any more (2:8.257). Dan realizes the only way he can forgive Anna is by confronting Larry.

Scene nine takes place one month later. Larry and Alice meet at a museum and we realize they have been lovers since their encounter at the lap dancing club in scene seven. It is Larry's birthday and Alice has bought him a Newton's Cradle. Her other surprise is to engineer a meeting between Anna and Larry. Also, in a scene reminiscent of their first encounter in scene two Anna returns the photographs she took of Alice. Despite a brief truce where the pair discuss the shortcomings of the two men they have shared, hostilities resume with Alice demanding that Anna give up Dan and return to Larry.

A second confrontation takes place one month later in scene ten between Dan and Larry. In the intervening period, Anna seems to have heeded Alice's advice to 'do the right thing' (2:10.269), and has gone back to Larry. Dan wants Anna back, but Larry uses the opportunity to crush his rival. Yet, while Larry discloses that he has slept with Alice, he also tells Dan where she can be found and advises that he go back to her again.

Scene eleven takes place one month later and appears at first to be a reconciliation between Dan and Alice. It is their anniversary and they quiz one another about details of their first meeting in scene one. However, Dan interrogates Alice based on his knowledge of Larry's brief affair with her. However, his insistence in attempting to extract the truth convinces Alice that she no longer loves Dan.

In scene twelve Anna and Larry meet in Postman's Park six months afterwards. Alice has unexpectedly died in a traffic accident back in New York. Larry and Anna have separated again and Larry is going out with a young nurse called Polly. Anna is now living alone in the countryside. Dan briefly joins Anna and Larry with the revelation that the name Alice Ayres was a pseudonym taken from one of the commemorative plaques in Postman's Park. 'Alice's' real name was Jane Jones. After this brief reunion all three characters '*exit separately*' (2:12.293).

Character analysis

A significant indication that *Closer* rejects psychological verisimilitude comes in the opening stage directions. Under the heading of 'characters' Marber includes the following: '**Alice**, *a girl from the town*. **Dan**, *a man from the suburbs*. **Larry**, *a man from the city*. **Anna**, *a woman from the country*' (182). The language and descriptions are loosely borrowed from Jacobean/Restoration drama in which character was often represented through type, and often based on class/social position rather than individual psychology. So while on the surface *Closer* seems realistic, conventional patterns of characterization are largely absent.

This mutability can be seen in the fluidity of identity, where none of the characters are what they seem. This extends from Alice's observation that 'Men want a girl who looks like a boy' (1:1.192), to the character of 'Anna' whom Dan anonymously adopts on the internet. It also manifests itself through Alice in ways that include concealment of her real name by adopting that of a dead Victorian heroine, to her appropriation in Dan's novel and Anna's photograph. Alice also lives through a further constructed identity via her occupation as a stripper.

Character development in the play is shown more as a form of slippage. When Alice seems not to reveal her true name in scene eight, Larry illustrates this process with his outburst: 'You think you haven't given us anything of yourselves . . . But you <u>do</u> give us something of yourselves' (2:7.249–50), where despite their tactics of evasion, at certain moments we get to understand something more about each character.

Not surprisingly, the person who most overtly displays these traits is Alice. Marber describes her as 'the soul of the play' (Marber 2001), yet this is difficult to define owing to the bewildering series of female archetypes she adopts – Victorian waif, loyal lover, temptress and victim: these roles are at times self-consciously adopted – while at other times imposed by others. The critic David Ian Rabey comments that it is this very 'indefinability' that lies at the heart of Alice's ability to attract and fascinate men, and with it 'ignite the imagination' (Rabey 2003: 200).

Alice's appropriation of whatever comes to hand in the construction of her identity not only includes the adoption by name of a dead Victorian girl, but circulates constantly in the different pasts she constructs through the scar on her leg. These stories are different for every person who asks, and range from an injury sustained by a truck (1:1.189) to a car accident in which both Alice's parents were killed (1:5.219).

Later in the play Larry's training as a dermatologist seems to get closer to both the origins of the scar as well as troubling hints about Alice's background through his suspicion that she might have created the scar herself in a condition called '*dermatitis artefacta* . . . a mental disorder manifested in the skin'. With reference to Alice's story of losing both her parents in a car crash Larry also comments that the condition is 'fairly common in children who lose their parents young' (2:10.273).

Whether Larry's observation is true or not, key to Alice's character is her essential isolation. From the very opening scene, on being asked by Dan if she wants to telephone anyone after the accident Alice comments, 'I don't know anyone' (1.1.185); later, Dan reveals to Anna that Alice 'has one address in her address book; ours ... under "H" for home' (1.2.198).

One possible symptom for this remoteness is her need to invent a myriad series of identities in order to disguise a lack of core identity. This is partially revealed to Anna in scene nine when Alice discloses that her obsession with Dan arises from the fact that 'he ... *buries* me. He makes me invisible' (2:9.267); and later in answer to Dan's demand to know who she is, Alice answers 'I'M NO ONE' (2:12.286).

Alice's behaviour is also defined by a contradictory series of impulses. At times she seems to display a complete lack of guile, commenting to Dan in the opening scene that the accident came about because 'I never look where I'm going' (1:1.185); yet in the encounter with Larry at the strip club in scene seven, she largely controls the situation in a series of elaborate displays of gamesmanship. Larry comments, 'You're cold' (2:7.250), yet while her death seems to cast her into the role of sacrificial victim, Alice also demonstrates throughout the play a capacity for a ruthless competitiveness. For instance, in scene five the moment Alice realizes that she is speaking to Anna's boyfriend, she '*moves in on him*' (1:5.217); in scene ten when Anna says she doesn't want a fight over Dan, Alice replies, 'SO GIVE IN' (2:9.266).

Alice's death also makes it tempting to read her character as essentially symbolic. The revelation that her Victorian namesake, 'by intrepid conduct saved three children ... at the cost of her own young life' (2:12.290), offers the audience a reading by which Alice has been sacrificed in the interests of the other three remaining characters. This interpretation, while providing a neat explanation, is also unsatisfactory to the point of one critic calling it the 'dangerously sentimental notion of the noble young stripper' (Winer 1999). One could also argue that this particular reading also proves unsatisfactory when one comes to consider exactly how Alice has 'saved' Dan, Larry and Anna, who seem to derive no benefit from her death and at the end all 'exit separately'(2:2.293). At times Marber seems to draw attention to these stereotypical associations by highlighting the fascination waifs exert on fiction of the period such as Dickens eponymous heroine in *Little Dorritt* (1855–7). A good example of this association is the incident in scene nine when we see Alice looking at the museum exhibit of '*a life-size model of a Victorian child . . . A girl dressed in rags*' (2:9.260).

However, Marber also seems to have set up a deliberate ambush for the unwary by using popular Victorian imagery that sentimentalized the poor in order to make a contemporary comparison between Anna's photography that also aestheticizes human suffering. Shortly after looking at her Victorian alter ego in the museum Alice meets Anna and is scathing about the morality of her photographic work, describing it as 'the beauty of ugliness' (2:9.265). While the neatly satisfying idea of Alice as Victorian waif persists until after her death – where Anna recounts how she has now adopted a stray mongrel dog (2:12.289) – Marber has commented that '[Alice is] not trying to kill herself; she was simply looking in the wrong direction while crossing the road' (Sierz 2000: 194).

If the character of Alice in Christopher Innes' words 'represents hope, not just as the waif-like idea of a male fantasy but as the fleeting chance for a meaningful relationship' (Innes 2002: 432), then Dan is far more a representative of the 'sterile and anatomized society' (Innes 2002: 435), that Innes also identities within the play. This can be seen in the opening scene where Dan's vocabulary is indicative of his personality: he comes from the 'graveyard' of suburbia (1.1.184) and works in the "Siberia" of journalism' (1:1.187). His occupation as an obituarist underscores his association with death and sterility.

We learn that the lives and characteristics of the deceased are encoded into euphemistic phrases by Dan and his fellow work colleagues: '"He valued his privacy" – gay' (1:1.188). Dan also provides a euphemism for himself: 'He was . . . *reserved* (1:1.189), yet just as the journalese most conceals their subjects' true proclivities, his apparent gentleness and concern towards Alice conceals a nature that is opportunistic and callous.

Dan's eventual decision to leave Alice in preference for Anna is not entirely surprising, for both share a trait of appropriating the lives of others for their own ends. Dan tells Alice in scene one, 'I had dreams of being a writer but I had no voice' (1:1.187), yet by the following scene he has used her life as the basis for his novel. As the critic Daniel Rosenthal succinctly observes, 'the Woolf devours the waif' (Marber 2007: xxxiii).

Similarly, Alice becomes incorporated into Anna's photographic exhibition as 'Young Woman, London', and later as a postcard for sale in a New York hotel lobby. Alice's demand for her negatives to be returned in scene nine becomes an act of recognition that Anna, despite protesting in scene two, 'I'm not a thief' (1:3.203) has taken something from her: earlier at the exhibition Alice also expresses her dislike of Anna's artistic appropriation of other peoples lives: 'It's a bunch of sad strangers photographed beautifully . . . But the people in the photos are sad and alone but the pictures make the world *seem* beautiful' (1:5.216).

Dan's parasitic nature is also revealed during his first meeting with Anna in scene two; he not only 'steals' her name and identity for his encounter on the internet in the following scene with Larry, but the appropriation even extends to the suggestion that they should meet at the Aquarium in London Zoo, a place Anna has told Dan she often visits. Her admiration for Dan's book being '*accurate*' (1:1.196) is also puzzling when the audience experience a sample of Dan's writing on the internet. Alice's later bitter rejoinder, 'Do you have a single original thought in your head' (2:11.286) is only too well demonstrated in his extensive borrowing from the hackneyed discourse of pornography in scene three, where Dan's performance as 'Anna' plays out familiar male clichés that depict women as creatures of voluptuous plenitude and erotic insatiability.

Dan's relationship with Alice also reveals contradictory attitudes towards her. In some respects Dan is reminiscent of figures in Jacobean City Comedy/Restoration Comedy in plays such as *Volpone* (1605–6) and *The Country Wife* (1675) that concern elderly men who jealously guard their young wives from potential suitors. This motif recurs in *Closer*, where in answer to Dan's comment that Alice is 'completely loveable and completely unleaveable', Anna believes Dan's true motives arise out of wanting to guard jealously Alice for himself – not because he loves her, but because 'you don't want someone else to get their dirty hands on her' (1:2.199).

Dan is essentially a weak character: while at one point urging Alice to disclose details of her affair with Larry because he is 'addicted' to the truth, in fact he remains just as much a 'known stranger' (2:11.283) to the term. At the same time Dan fails to disclose information to others if it will become detrimental to his own self-interests. For instance, we only learn at the very end that on the day of his first encounter with Alice, his crustless sandwiches that morning were a sheer coincidence because, 'the bread . . . *broke* in my hands' (2:12.292). Dan deliberately fails to disclose this particular piece of information to Alice earlier, precisely because he knows this to be the principal reason why she '*chose*' him (2:9.267).

Although he makes a brief appearance in the opening scene, shares the stage with Dan in scene three via the internet and inadvertently meets the real Anna at London Zoo in scene four, Larry is not fully involved in the lives of the other three characters until scene five at the opening of Anna's exhibition. While Larry likes to remind Anna, 'you forget you're dealing with a clinical observer of the human carnival' (1:6.225), in many respects he does not share the dispassionate qualities of the other characters and is far quicker to feel emotions such as grief and anger. He also harbours grudges more passionately than the others.

In part this appears to stem from class differences. While nowhere as pronounced as *After Miss Julie*, despite his status as a consultant dermatologist, Larry is sensitive about his working class background. For instance, at Anna's exhibition Larry compares himself to 'Cinderella at the ball', to which Anna responds, 'You're such a peasant' (1:6.224). Also, in a moment reminiscent of *After Miss Julie*, when after their sexual liaison John can now claim his one time mistress, Anna observes that Larry looks 'like "the cat who got the cream"' (1:6.225); this remark upsets Larry deeply as he recognizes that it is a thinly disguised reference to differences in their social class, and a few lines afterwards he asks whether Anna's parents 'didn't think I was "beneath you"'? (1:6.225).

Larry's inner conflict also shows in his discomfort within a variety of alien environments. These range from his unfamiliarity in the virtual world of cyberspace (1:3.204) and his embarrassing first meeting with Anna at the Aquarium in scene four, and Anna's later surprise in seeing him at a museum (2:9.261). However, Larry's class anxieties become most apparent in his attitude towards the expensive new apartment he and Anna have moved into after their marriage, and he concludes that working class guilt is the reason why every time he visits 'the *Elle Decoration* bathroom . . . I feel *dirty* . . . It's got <u>attitude</u>. The mirror says, "Who the fuck are you?"' (1:6.228).

Whether class tensions are the cause, out of all the characters in the play Larry is the most openly competitive and overtly 'masculine' in his outlook. A telling instance comes from his early resentment towards Dan, both for being duped on the internet in scene three as well as Dan's continuing attraction to Anna. Larry expresses both these insecurities through the most basic form of masculine aggression: 'I could 'ave 'im . . . If it came to a scrap, I could 'ave 'im' (1:6.224), although in the end Larry proves far more successful in destroying Dan through guile than brute force by persuading Anna for a 'final fuck' (2:8.254), in return for her freedom to marry Dan. Larry knows that by doing so Dan will eventually find out, and so destroy his own relationship with Anna. As he explains to Dan: 'I fucked her to fuck you up', and although their confrontation does not result in a fist-fight, Larry asserts that 'a good fight is never clean' (2:10.271).

Patrick Marber has commented, 'For me, *Closer* is about people who tell the truth' (Sierz 2001: 193), and it is Larry who best epitomizes this quality. While Dan tells Anna, 'what's so great about the truth?' (2:8.255) after her revelation about the one-off '*sympathy* fuck', with her estranged husband (2:8.256), it is Larry who seems most obsessed by questions of honesty. As mentioned, his insistence on knowing the full sexual details of Anna's betrayal comes from a sense of masochistic martyrdom, yet at other times – such as paying over £500 for Alice to confirm her real name – reveals a genuine need for total disclosure and leads to his outburst in the controlled environment of the lap dancing club, 'WHAT D'YOU HAVE TO DO TO GET A BIT OF INTIMACY AROUND HERE?' (2:8.250).

Although Alice is usually seen as the character who is most associated with the quality of unknowability, it could be argued that it is Anna who remains the most enigmatic character in *Closer*. Like Alice, her nebulous identity is hinted at early on in her first meeting with Dan when she hesitates about whether she is still married, replying first 'Yes' and then 'No' to Dan's question (1:2.198). As mentioned, her capacity to appropriate the lives of others in her photographic work makes her *simpatico* with Dan – the critic Daniel Rosenthal calls this 'the photographic equivalent of one-night stands' (Marber 2007: xli); yet Anna also demonstrates on occasions an amoral pragmatism, as in her decision to sleep with Larry one last time for the expediency of a quick divorce settlement. While this revelation is devastating to Dan, Anna justifies her action with the phrase 'It was only _sex_' (2:8.257), in language that borrows from associations traditionally ascribed to men in relation to casual infidelity.

Anna's attraction as an artist to projects that include photographing strangers and derelict buildings allude to her own sense of isolation. When Larry encounters her at the Aquarium she has gone there alone on her birthday, and in the final scene she has retreated to the country and bought a dog for company. While Larry urges, 'Don't become . . . a sad person', Anna responds, 'I won't. I'm not' (2:12.289), yet it is she who mentions the collection of poems entitled Solitude – a condition she seems destined to embrace indefinitely.

Influences and genre

Like the shape of the question mark that constitutes Alice's scar, _Closer_ paradoxically defines itself by constantly eluding and contradicting easy definitions made for it belonging to a specific genre: so while it has a structure that is formalized and intricate, it never quite belongs to the form defined by the 'well-made play' due to its moments of brutal and explosive emotion; similarly, while it has been described as a comedy its overall themes are mostly bleak and pessimistic. The play also shares certain features associated with the sub-genre Comedy of Manners, where aspects of modern life shape human behaviour and conduct. This is illustrated most notably with the internet encounter in scene three and its impact on patterns of courtship.

While _Closer_ seems to take its basic plot device – two couples swapping partners over the course of the play – from Noel Cowards' _Private Lives_ (1933), its influences are a good deal more ambiguous and multifarious, and limits of space only allow a relatively brief mention of its principal influences. While Marber has always been forthcoming in this respect, particularly regarding the influence that Pinter and Mamet, as well as Stephen Soderbergh's film *Sex, Lies and Videotape* (1989), critics have also attributed a whole host of other influences to *Closer*. These have ranged from Luigi Pirandello's *Naked* (1918–22), to Robert Altman's film *Short-cuts* (1993), based on the short stories of Raymond Carver.

One source of the embryonic ideas that were subsequently developed in *Closer* was Marber's own 1995 television adaptation of Strindberg's *Miss Julie*. As Richard Eyre comments, 'It was said of *Closer* that the play had echoes of Strindberg, but it's more that Strindberg had leaked into *Closer*' (Marber 2004: xiii), while Peter Buse observes that the adaptation with its 'sudden shifts from tenderness to venomous exchanges . . . anticipates the concerns of [Marber's] next play, *Closer* . . . which like *Miss Julie* mediates on the inherent reversibility of desire' (Buse 2006). However, while John and Miss Julie's feelings for each other veer back and forth between extremes of love and hatred after sexual consummation, the reversibility of desire in *Closer* is more controlled. As mentioned earlier, Alice changes rapidly from professing that she 'would've loved [Dan] forever' (2:11.285), to knowing the exact moment she has fallen out of love with him. Similarly, the scene opens with Dan stroking Alice (2:11.278), and ends with him slapping Alice across the face (2:11.286). Both *After Miss Julie* and *Closer* ends with the deaths of their female protagonists, and while John comments, 'We kill what we love' (130), Alice's death through a car accident is less melodramatic than Miss Julie's suicide.

An early review of *Closer* described it as a version of Noel Coward's '*Private Lives* for the Nineties' (Coveney 1997), and Marber has acknowledged, 'I suppose it's an intimate comedy like *Private Lives* about people who can't live with each other but who can't live without each other' (Gardner 1998). In either a quirk of programming, or recognition of its similarities, the year that *Closer* transferred to Broadway, the Royal National Theatre staged a revival of *Private Lives* directed by Philip Franks – and in 2001 the relationship was made even more unambiguous with Jonathan Church's production at the Birmingham Repertory Theatre which put *Closer* and *Private Lives* in repertoire as a way of encouraging direct comparison. Dominic Cavendish found the pairing complementary: 'Watching the two plays in succession, you get a thrilling insight into the way two writers handle the same thorny subject – the restlessness of male/female desire – with an accent on their own times.' He also saw both plays belonging to the quintessentially English tradition of the 'well-made play': 'Both plays put wit at a premium and both take delight in artifice, marshalling the chaotic charge of emotions into neat structural symmetries' (Cavendish 2001).

Other critics, including Alastair Macaulay, also felt that the structure of *Closer* derived from a classical antecedent – Jean Racine's *Andromaque* (1667). Here 'A loves B, B loves C, C loves D. However, when C decides to marry B, A's suffering is extreme' (Macaulay 1998). Michael Raab also finds the comparison convincing owing to Marber's direction in 1996 of a stage adaptation of Craig Raine's poem *1953* (1990), which in turn was a loose adaptation of Racine's play. The critic Daniel Rosenthal notes that '*Closer* echoes the rhythms and raw imagery of Raine's verse as it explores the selfishness of desire' (Marber 2007: xiv), while Marber himself has acknowledged that the structure of *Closer* emerged from his practical engagement with Raine's poem: 'I perceived the shape of it very profoundly . . . the centre of it [1953] is two men and two women who all love each other in various combinations . . . so I was given the shape of *Closer*, really, for free by Craig's play' (Marber 2007: xvi).

The structure of *Closer* also drew comparisons with Harold Pinter's play *Betrayal* (1978), and Marber's own career has demonstrated an ongoing practical engagement with Pinter's theatre. While *Closer* chooses to look at the parallel and intersecting infidelities of its four characters from the beginning, rather than the same course of events over a single affair; both plays share broadly similar themes such as the anatomization of pain and guilt that arises from infidelity and shared, yet different memories of the past. Likewise, several critics have also pointed out the likenesses between the two plays in terms of their shared rhythms, patterning in language as well as the formal and symmetrical balance of its scenes

Again, either through accident or design, in 1998 audiences were given the opportunity to draw upon comparisons between the two plays when, during *Closer*'s residency in the West End the Royal National Theatre staged a revival of *Betrayal*, which even featured the actress Imogen Stubbs who had previously played Anna in *Closer*.

Close reading of key scenes

As mentioned, *Closer* shares several features of the archetypically 'well-made play', where chronologically scenes allude not only to future events, but also refer back to the past; even while relying on significant coincidences such as Anna happening to be at London Zoo at exactly same time Larry is waiting to rendezvous with the 'Nymph of the Net' (1:4.209), *Closer* avoids many of the clichés associated with this style of playwriting. The close associations between discrete scenes and its overall structure make it difficult to single out specific scenes for analysis, but the three chosen examples demonstrate significant interconnections that can be found between its overall structure.

Act 1, Scene 1

The opening scene is the fulcrum on which *Closer* rests, for it not only introduces the predominant themes and ideas of the play but gives significant intimations of future events. The opening exchanges between Alice and Dan seem on the surface to be a flirtatious preamble to courtship, yet several other important discourses run through their conversation.

For instance, beneath the teasing and witty dialogue runs the recurrent motif of death, where Alice's injury in the traffic accident prefigures news of her death under exactly the same circumstances in the last scene of the play. Other references to Alice's premature end include Dan in his capacity as a newspaper obituarist providing her one sentence epitaph, to Alice's final moments linking back to her first meeting with Dan: 'We stood at the lights, I looked into your eyes and then you . . . stepped in the road' (1:1.185).

Human mortality haunts this scene in other ways. Dan has moved from the 'graveyard' of suburbia (1:1.184) to work as a journalist memorializing public figures; Alice reminds Dan that his age at thirty-five is 'half-time' (1:1.186), and discloses that prior to the accident she had been watching 'the carcasses' being unloaded (1:1.187) at Smithfield Market. Even Alice's habit of smoking is contrasted against the story of the death of Dan's mother, who he pointedly comments 'was a smoker' (1:1.187).

Human transience in scene one is also linked to place not only via the hospital and Smithfield's meat market but also by another key location that is introduced in the opening scene – Postman's Park. Alice's comment, 'it's a graveyard too' (1:1.187) is perceptive, for the memories and events associated with this specific location connects all the characters. The memorial (which actually exists) was set up by the Victorian painter G. F. Watts for the purpose Alice outlines. Her cryptic line which immediately follows, 'It's most *curious*' (1:1.187) possibly alludes to the revelation that is kept for the last scene of the play, where Dan discovers she has assumed the name of Alice Ayres from one of the names memorialized on the plaques at Watt's memorial.

The circumstances of Dan and Alice's first meeting assume importance from the start: even as events directly unfold Alice wants Dan to construct the immediate past – the moments she been rendered unconscious by the accident – into the form of a narrative. This detailed storytelling of events is later repeated much later in scene eleven, where the couple's first encounter becomes the central focus around which their fourth anniversary is celebrated; here each quizzes the other over minute details associated around their initial meeting at the hospital.

Ironically it this concern with recounting the events of scene one that ends up severing their relationship irrevocably. These problems emerge early on when Dan mixes up his memories of Alice's account about crossing Blackfriars Bridge (1.1.186) with Anna's story in the next scene about the secret river and the swimming pig (1:2.194). Their reminiscences also raise the spectre of Larry who made a brief appearance in the scene to examine Alice's leg. Alice's subsequent illicit affair with Larry, and Dan's insistence on testing her over his secret knowledge of the liaison cause Alice to finally leave him for good. Yet, even this final break in their relationship is alluded to in scene one, where Alice's curt, 'I don't love you any more. Goodbye' (2:11.284) to Dan matches exactly the story she tells him about suddenly leaving a previous lover in New York prior to the beginning of the play (1:1.191).

Other details from the opening scene also assume significance later on. In scene nine Alice discloses to Anna that she initially '*chose*' Dan at the hospital for the most unlikely of reasons: 'I looked in his briefcase and I found this . . . sandwich . . . and I thought, "I will give all my love to this charming man who cuts off his crusts"' (2:9.267). Even the sandwiches' content – fish – becomes noteworthy later. For instance, in the following scene Anna suggests 'The Aquarium' as a better title for Dan's book, which in turn becomes the rendezvous point at London Zoo in scene four for Larry and Anna's first meeting.

The other central image that the opening scene introduces, and which reverberates throughout the play is the motif of flesh and the meanings of surfaces. Its first introduction is through the wound on Alice's leg; later this is contrasted with Alice's story about watching the butchered animal carcasses being unloaded at Smithfield Market – a spectacle which despite finding 'repulsive' (1:1.187), she feels compelled to watch: Alice has recently left one meat market – a New York strip club to observe a real one in London. Moreover, her position in the role of spectator also reverses the dynamics of her job as a stripper – another type of 'meat market', where her flesh is also openly on display to paying customers.

Skin imagery also manifests itself in the opening scene by the ambiguous scar on Alice's leg. Larry, a dermatologist also 'in the skin trade' (2:7.244) examines it '*with interest*' (1:1.189). His initial action of tracing its line with his finger (1:1.189) begins a process that develops throughout the play whereby his fascination with the scar (which Alice later tells Anna that he licks it, 'like a dog' (2:10.268)), also becomes an attempt to decode her character.

The other principal theme of appropriation in *Closer* is also introduced in the opening scene. Although Dan is honest enough to realize that as a writer he has 'no voice' (1:1.187), he later ventriloquizes Alice's language in their first encounter – such as her phrase 'come . . . like a *train*' (1:1.192) when he later poses as 'Anna' on the internet (1:3.207). Their initial meeting also persuades Dan to make Alice the subject of his novel. These two forces of appropriation and seduction vie for each other throughout the scene and it is of little surprise that by scene two Dan and Alice have entered into a relationship.

Act 1, Scene 3

The internet scene in *Closer* has simultaneously been described as both 'aggressively contemporary' (Innes 2002: 433), yet at the same time 'never fails to bring the house down' with its 'masterfully . . . traditional comic techniques of misrecognition and disguise' (Buse 2006). Certainly it is the one scene that initially attracted most attention by critics and audiences, and in some respects has come to define *Closer*.

As mentioned, on one level it is a hugely enjoyable piece of theatre, although the characters of Larry and Dan sit separately and silently on either side of the stage with their written comments to each other displayed on a large overhead screen. As also mentioned, the scene was an early theatrical response to depicting the relatively new technological innovation of the internet. This in turn produced the challenge of finding ways to stage the scene. Emma B. Lloyd, who was assistant stage manager on the original Royal National Theatre production, recalls that a significant problem quickly presented itself during technical rehearsals:

> The first time we tried to run the Internet scene, it took the actors 40 minutes to type the dialogue. Patrick and I tried it later and got it down to 20, but of course that was still hopeless. In the end we had to get a special computer programme written with the whole script on the programme. So though it looks real, the actors are only pretending to type. How it works is that I watch them very carefully and when they touch the first key for a sentence I activate a quick key which makes the whole thing appear on the big screen above their heads. The entire scene now takes six minutes. (Gardner 1998)

Despite the now universal presence of the internet, re-evaluating the scene today shows that it was not just included for its novelty value, but is integral to the play's overall theme and mood. For one, it represents – albeit in an exaggerated comic fashion – the apogee of Dan's willingness to appropriate the identities of others for his own ends. In the previous scene we have learnt that Alice has become the subject of his novel, and now his current obsession with Anna has prompted the creation of a fictional 'Anna' whom

Dan can construct and manipulate as he wishes via the anonymity of the internet.

While apparently consisting of only of two men statically typing their responses to one another onstage, the scene also displays an innovative and self-conscious theatricality within this seemingly 'well-made play'. Marber describes the scene as an updating of Shakespeare's *Twelfth Night*.

> The idea of the disconnected city was continued in the internet scene, the second scene I wrote. I think of it as a *Twelfth Night* 'breeches scene' in reverse. Very Shakespearean. (Gardner 1998)

It is this convention of cross-gendering, borrowed from Elizabethan theatre, and its practical application through the technology of the internet that makes the scene both startlingly original, yet also completely at home in the medium of theatre. Like Shakespearian comedy that employs cross-dressing, much of the humour derives from the knowingness of the audience as to the true identifies of the gender impostor(s) against the ignorance of others onstage. Marber has commented, 'The scene only works because Larry is a net virgin' (Sierz 2001: 193), and the device of cross-dressing is realized 'virtually' by way of the anonymity afforded by the internet; consequently Dan is not only able to retain his male gender onstage but can simultaneously pose as 'Anna' to Larry with the audience aware of both personas during the performance.

Yet while Marber departs from the traditional physical exaggeration that accompanies males adopting a cross-dressing role, he provides it through the discourse utilized in the scene. Dan's construction of 'Anna' comes via the clichéd language of men's pornographic writing, which, as Daniel Rosenthal observes, produces a construction of women who 'crave nothing more than group sex with strangers, including simultaneous vaginal and anal penetration' (Marber 2007: xliv). Subsequently, 'Anna' depicts herself to

Larry in the following terms: 'Dark hair. Dirty mouth. Epic tits' (1:3.204), and who sexually services a group of male strangers, 'like a cum hungry bitch, 1 in each hole and both hands' (2:3.206).

Marber also sees the scene as important in showing a certain aspect of male sexuality:

> Originally I wrote it between a man and a woman, but then I realized I was missing a trick and could show undiluted male fantasy at work, get really plugged into their libidos. (Gardner 1998)

Male cross-dressing often hints at a certain latent homosexuality, and the scene provides a theatricalized illustration of Alice's observation in the opening scene that 'Men want a girl who looks like a boy' (1:1.192). While the relationship between Carl and Ash in Marber's previous play, *Dealer's Choice* implied an unrequited interest from the older man, in *Closer* it is only by recourse to the internet that Dan is able to vicariously explore any homoerotic fantasies; when in the previous scene Dan jokily replies that like Anna he does not kiss strange men (1:2.198), we see him 'virtually' doing this (and far more!) in the next scene with Larry.

Alice's summary of men's perfect woman in the opening scene – androgynous, tough, but in need of protection, sexually voracious but simultaneously poised in their enjoyment (1:1.192) – finds some realization in Dan's portrayal of 'Anna'. Yet, the newspaper critic Paul Taylor, reviewing the play after it transferred to the Lyttleton at the Royal National Theatre, felt that Dan's brief habitation as a woman is deliberately rendered unconvincing. As mentioned, part of the reason for this is that 'Anna' is a composite of clichés gathered from the annals of pornographic writing – the products of what Larry later calls men's 'Home Movies . . . the shit that slops through our minds every day'(2:8.250). Dan's version of Anna becomes a man-made creation that encompasses what men ideally want a woman to be. This leads Taylor to believe that the scene demonstrates, 'Marber's priority . . . to show how women are significantly absent in this most skewed but most successful exchange of intimacies in the play' (Taylor 1997).

Although the internet scene played a significant part in *Closer* winning the Evening Standard Award for Best Comedy in 1997, and despite its comic exchanges it is amongst the bleakest in the play. Marber himself has expressed surprise at how the scene became something of a comic set-piece: 'It gets more laughs than I anticipated. When I wrote it, I thought it was rather disturbing' (Gardner 1998).

In a later exchange that is meant to be comic, Anna on learning of the internet encounter comments on the scene's essential sterility – describing it as 'two boys tossing in cyber-space' (1:5.212). David Ian Rabey goes further by commenting that the scene, 'is also a wry demonstration of how technology does not "shrink the world", but maintain[s] and extend[s] the distance between people' (Rabey 2003: 199). Dan's comment, 'We liv [sic] as we dream, ALONE' (1:3.207) establishes a condition beyond the virtual environment of the internet.

This sense of human isolation is compounded further, when even the chance of brief connection through solitary, yet simultaneous acts of masturbation are denied the two men. Larry is deterred by a fear of being caught at his workplace, and Dan fakes his orgasm by representing it as a random outburst of letters and strokes on the computer keyboard (1:3.206). However, the deception practised in Dan's virtual orgasm is later humorously revisited when he is wounded to learn that in the past Anna has periodically faked sexual climax during their lovemaking (2:8.256).

The inherent bleakness of this ambiguously comic scene is reinforced during a moment when Larry is interrupted by a phone call, and while we are not privy to its content his comment, 'What's the histology? *Progressive?* Sounds like an atrophy'

(1:3.205), makes the exchange sounds as if it is a diagnosis following a pathology report for a skin cancer, which reaffirms the dominant connections in *Closer* between human desire, sexuality and death.

Act 2, Scene 7

Patrick Marber reveals that the genesis for this scene – and the first actually written for the play – came about after visiting an American lap dancing club when *Dealer's Choice* was on tour in the city of Atlanta:

> The experience was akin to the very first time that I walked into a casino. A disturbing strangeness . . . I started writing that scene and the rest of the play formed either side of it. (Gardner 1998)

The scene in question shows a chance encounter between Alice and Larry at a strip club, where the former works. Both have lost their respective partners in the previous scene, yet rather than mutually commiserating, an elaborate charade is played out involving Alice pretending not to know Larry and Larry trying to ascertain Alice's true identity.

As with so much in *Closer*, prior references to this scene have already been well prepared. We know for instance from the opening scene that Alice works as a stripper, and in scene three Dan tells Larry via the internet that 'PARADISE SHOULD BE SHOCKING' (1:3.207). However, 'The Paradise Suite' (2:7.240) where the encounter between Alice and Larry takes place is anything but spontaneous or shocking. Christopher Innes calls it 'a commercialized delusion' (Innes 2002: 433) and 'paradise' is revealed to be six identically named suites that are strictly controlled by a set of rules that govern allowable conduct between dancer and client, in an environment under constant surveillance by cameras.

The scene also provides a useful checklist in a critique which has come to be known as Postmodernism. While definitions for this umbrella term are somewhat nebulous, the scene does serve to demonstrate one of its key features – namely how the lap dancing club is deliberately constructed to blur the subject's own sense of identity: these include the constant scrutiny of Alice and Larry through technology and a commodification of sexuality into a series of transactions between consumers and human 'products' as well as a breakdown in the demarcation between what is real and fake through both replication.

These features are constantly alluded to throughout the scene. For instance, Larry finds the club a bewildering place, unsure of its rules and codes of conduct and haunted by the fact that the building has changed its appearance and purpose. He recalls, 'I used to come here twenty years ago . . . it was a punk club' and he concludes, 'Everything is a Version of Something Else' (2:7.240). Larry also remembers that, 'I went to a place like this in New York' (2:7.241), and it soon becomes clear that the lap dancing club is an example of the term *globalization*, where a chain of identical establishments from America (in much the same way as fast-food outlets), has been transplanted and relocated to Britain. In equally sardonic terms Larry comments that the process, with its 'swish' environment is something to be welcomed: 'Pornography has gone upmarket – BULLY FOR ENGLAND. This is honest *progress* don't you think?' Alice's enigmatic reply, 'England always imports the best of America' (2:7.241) does little to convince that such cloning is a positive aspect of modernity.

Yet Alice also subsumes her identity as part of the club's brand and ideology: when asked by Larry what her pudenda tastes of, she describes it using the term 'Heaven' (2:7.241), a corporate simile based on the name of the suite in which she performs for customers. This sublimation of identity eventually leads to her temporarily failing to distinguish the difference between the rules governing the club and those of the outside world: in scene eleven when Alice threatens to call security and eject Dan from their hotel room, he points out, 'You're not in a strip club. There is no security' (2:11.285).

The ersatz environment of the lap dancing club also leads to Larry being unable to distinguish the differences between truth and deception. At first he is able to spot some of the deliberate falsehoods that operate in the club such the *nom de plum* 'Cupid' that one of the girls adopts, because 'Cupid was a bloke' (2:7.246). Previously this had been the nickname Anna and Larry gave to Dan as a private joke (1:6.224), and at first Larry demonstrates a satisfaction in appropriating the nickname for Dan. However, Alice corrects Larry by saying, 'He wasn't a bloke, he was a little boy' (2:7.246). From this point onwards a process begins whereby Larry starts to become increasingly unable to distinguish truth from reality. This reaches its climax in his bid to know Alice's real name – even when he pays increasingly large sums of money for the answer. Alice's reply of 'Jane Jones' (2:7.246) refuses to provide the confirmation he requires, and Larry still prefers to believe that her identity resides under the false credentials of Alice Ayres.

This obsession with names reverberates throughout the scene. Larry himself even plays out the same deception at the beginning of their encounter when he calls himself 'Daniel' (2:7.245) as a way of goading Alice into admitting that she knows him. He also bitterly concludes that the aliases assumed by the other lap dancers comes from another reason: 'You all use "stage names" to con yourselves you're someone else so you don't feel *ashamed* when you show your *cunts* and *arseholes* to Complete Fucking Strangers (2:7.247).

Marber describes the scene as 'an extraordinary baachanalian whirlpool of complex power relationships' (Sierz 2001: 191), and in paying to asecertain something so basic as someone's real name Larry has quickly become ensnared by the club's intention to define human interaction to a series of commercial transactions, regardless of whether they have any meaning. Alice defines these terms: 'You're the customer, I'm the service' (2:7.249), but the 'service' does not include any form of touching nor sharing of genuine human contact. Larry points out the paradox to Alice that while ostensibly divesting her clothes she still wears 'armour' (2:7.244).

As the scene progresses, far from entering the Paradise Suite, for Larry the place soon comes to represent a Miltonic 'hellhole' (2:7.247). For its characters and the audience, Larry's resentment at his inability to take control of Alice through their relationship of client and service comes early on in the scene – between complimenting Alice for having 'the face of an angel', he next asks the boorish question, 'What does your cunt taste like?' (2:7.241).

From that point onwards the pair engage in a war of attrition which is different for both. Larry wishes to reveal his true feelings at the loss of Anna and at the same time confirm that Alice reciprocates in kind about Dan. In contrast, Alice attempts to conceal as much about herself as possible, although paradoxically she does reveal her real name, which Larry chooses not to believe – when Alice declares 'it's not a war', Larry's only response is to '*laugh . . . for some time*' (2:8.250). However, it is a battle which Larry ultimately seems destined to lose as he not only admits to his own sense of pain and rejection by Anna, but resorts to threatening Alice with violence when she still refuses to give anything of herself away to him (2:7.249).

Larry then makes two statements that reveal much about himself and masculinity in general. In one instance he rejects Alice's unobtainable status to himself and the other clients in the lap dancing club because she has given them '*imagery* . . . and we do with it what we will'. He then goes on to make a generalized but chilling remark about his own gender: 'If you women could see one minute of our Home Movies – the shit that slops through our minds every day – you'd string us up by our balls, you really would'

(2:7.250). This expression of what Marber calls 'the uncensored male libido' (Sierz 2001: 193) is explored earlier in scene three via Dan and Larry's pornographic missives over the internet, and it even informs Marber's previous play *After Miss Julie*, where the eponymous protagonist realizes that John will use events from their sexual consummation in the same way Larry suggests in *Closer*: 'Look at you, you can't believe it, can you? You're still reliving it in your head, your dirty little film in your dirty little fleapit of a mind' (164).

The incident also serves to recall a further comment Larry makes to Alice in the club: 'You don't understand the territory because you *are* the territory' (2:8.250). With its associations of hunting and prey, it gives the impression that little real emotional understanding exists between the sexes, with men responding to women purely in terms of their sexuality.

While this reveals on the one hand a masculinity that is highly manipulative and misogynistic, there is also another equal strand constructed around a deep sense of self-loathing. Larry asks at one point, whether many of the men who visit the club end up 'crying their guts out', to which Alice replies, 'Occupational hazard' (2:7.248).

David Ian Rabey points out that, 'significantly and artfully, we never actually see the character (or performer) of Alice strip' (Rabey 2003: 200) during the scene; this ambiguity is made explicit in the latest published edition of *Closer* where Marber has excised the stage direction at the end of the scene, '**Alice** *looks straight at him and begins to undress, slowly*' (Marber 1997, *Closer*: 67).

However, Larry believes that Alice's nakedness as she strips for him does unwittingly reveal her inner feelings (2:8.250). This idea of the body betraying its psyche reoccurs in the following scene when Anna, confessing to Dan that she slept with Larry in a bid to win her divorce, justifies the infidelity: 'I didn't give *him* anything' (2:8.255). However, Dan's shock at this revelation comes from the fact that he understands only too well that a sexual transaction between two people can never be entirely clinical.

Like the representation of the internet earlier, Marber uses the properties of theatre to accentuate the voyeurism of the lap dancing environment in this scene. He has also commented that one way of analysing the play is to see Anna, Larry and Dan as 'lookers' and Alice as 'looked at' (Sierz 2001: 188); here it is through the 'liveness' of striptease as performance that Alice particularly becomes objectified by the theatre audience who also become hidden spectators at this supposedly private showing that Alice performs for Larry as a paying customer. David Ian Rabey also points out that the 1999 Royal National Theatre production emphasized this sense of voyeurism by a back projection of Alice and Larry taken from one of the surveillance cameras in the ceiling (Rabey 2003: 200).

The scene also self-consciously draws attention to the invisible 'fourth wall' that situates the audience when Alice draws Larry's attention to their activities being monitored by cameras. Here, Alice '*nods in the direction of the audience*' (2:7.244) to alert Larry to the fact that the 'fourth wall' is represented by a two-way mirror. David Ian Rabey observes that Larry's address to the mirror/ audience, 'WHAT D'YOU HAVE TO GET A BIT OF INTIMACY AROUND HERE?' (2:8.250) becomes a highly theatrical act as it 'both acknowledges and momentarily blasts the fiction of the invisible audience' (Rabey 2003: 200). Peter Buse also sees Larry's outburst as illustrative of a key theme in *Closer* – namely, 'the restless hunt for intimacy' (Buse 2006), and points out that despite being in an environment that seems to promise it, in fact the lap dancing club denies any chance of engaging meaningfully with another person.

Changing Views of the Play

Aleks Sierz summarizes the initial critical response to *Closer* being 'a case of love at first sight' (Sierz 2001: 188), and the play was notable for the almost unanimous critical praise received after its London and Broadway debuts. Superlatives ranged from 'the one English play in years which successfully plumbs those lower depths of the human personality' (De Jongh 1998), to 'the writing is so accomplished, it seems almost unfair to point to its faults' (Benedict 1997).

However, as early as October 1997, after transferring to the bigger Lyttleton stage, Paul Taylor used the opportunity to reassess *Closer*'s lionization. One of his chief criticisms concerned the play being a less intense emotional experience than it had first appeared; instead it more resembled 'a piece of human algebra . . . calculated to within an inch of its mannered staccato Pinter-ish life' (Taylor 1997). A similar comment was also made by one of the reviewers of the New York production who concluded that, 'In the end *Closer* is too satisfied with its own dark vision to risk any real emotion [which] makes it ultimately as cold and self-absorbed as its characters ' (O'Toole 1999).

The theatre director Dominic Dromgoole was rather more cutting in his assessment of Marber's work in general, comparing it to the effects of cocaine in which 'you find yourself being brilliantly articulate about a few tiny platitudes, so Marber manages to make some fairly thin truisms seem like great profundities' (Dromgoole 2000: 194). Like Taylor, Dromgoole seems to be saying that critics and audiences were only all too ready to be seduced by the dazzling surface of *Closer* which has resulted in 'a brilliant boulevard entertainer [being] held up as a major artist' (Dromgoole 2000: 195).

Critics Aleks Sierz and Ken Urban both observe that a preoccupation with appearances became a significant feature of many new British plays from the 1990s. Sierz cites Jez Butterworth's *Mojo* as a key example, in which 'the play's highly charged surface glitter takes priority over plot, character, or depth' (Sierz 1998: 332). Urban however argues that below the stylish, depthless surface of many of the plays associated with 'Cool Britannia' lurked what he terms 'Cruel Britannia' – a form of nihilism predicated on allowing the possibility of transformation (Urban 2004: 355). As mentioned in the opening chapter, it is easy to view *Closer* initially as a stylish yet shallow work; yet arguably the play is far nearer to Urban's definition of 'Cruel' rather than 'Cool', where its seeming preoccupation with surfaces – Alice's name, her scar and photographic image for instance – disguises a more complex agenda.

Another criticism of *Closer* concerned an aspect of its success: namely its honesty at exposing the rawness of sexual betrayal, the failure of individuals to communicate and its refusal to provide 'a happy ending', which Christopher Innes sees as best expressed through the inability of any of the characters to produce children, implying that the society in *Closer* 'literally has no future' (Innes 2002: 433). However, Innes' chief criticism is also connected to its ending and the lack of an 'explicit political statement of the kind marking the earlier generation of playwrights like [Howard] Brenton, [David] Edgar and [David] Hare' (Innes 2002: 433). For Innes, Marber and his 1990s' contemporaries 'give[s] no sense that [the millennium] will bring change' (Innes 2002: 435). The critic Michael Billington echoed this sentiment, and while still praising *Closer* concluded it only ever 'fleetingly relates sex to society' (Billington 1997). Dominic Dromgoole was again more damning, and accused Marber's work of offering his largely comfortable West End and Broadway audiences 'a chaos filled with violence, sexual desire and sexual disgust, and endless mutual loathing' (Dromgoole 2000: 195), in order to produce what Dromgoole elsewhere has termed *fake pain*:

We live in a world of rampant cruelty, waste and injustice; we see it in every place, at every level . . . Yet in theatre, this didn't stop wealthy, healthy, middle-class folk looking at some inane subject like pensions or architecture or spying or newspapers and finding more rottenness than in any Denmark, more pain than in any holocaust, more apocalypse than any Hiroshima. (Bradwell 1997: 73)

The critic Klaus Peter Müller also comments that this 'sense of relish in the destructive and dehumanizing worlds' depicted in much 1990s' drama also 'seemed to be particularly marketable . . . indeed [was] often regarded as especially entertaining' (Müller 2002: 15, 17) and also argues that against this sense of pessimism and relish for cruelty in plays from the period, 'the amount of direct political statements is . . . rather small' (Müller 2002: 15).

It could also be argued that *Closer* and other plays from the period which explored relationships and sexuality were merely doing so in order to avoid an engagement with politics. The television series *This Life* has already been mentioned in connection with *Closer*, where it could be said that it is the relationships themselves which take precedence over an engagement with society. The critic Glen Crebber points out that this also became a major criticism of *This Life* in that it 'reflected a world where politics itself was concentrated as much with the moral construction of self-identity as with wider social and political issues' (Creeber 2004: 122).

However, such criticism fails to take into account Marber's own views on his writing which seems to privilege feeling and experience over political analysis:

All you can do as an artist is say 'I was there and this is what it felt like'. And I thought: that's the kind of artist I want to be – to document experience, with some feeling. Of course there are other artists who say 'nonsense, your job is political, or your job is to reflect your age'. (www.ramagazine.org.uk)

While this stance seems to place Marber amongst dramatists such as Tom Stoppard, Simon Gray and Alan Bennett rather than David Hare, Howard Brenton and David Edgar, Marber's adaptation of *After Miss Julie* is arguably far more overtly 'political' than Strindberg's original in terms of its transference to post-war England: in Marber's version it becomes more a battle between class than gender; as Christopher Innes points out, this 'explicitly political play' with its 'caustic and uncomfortable analysis underlies the apparently neutral portrayal of contemporary life in his comedies' (Innes 2002: 431).

Genre, structure and language

The first significant attempt at classifying Marber's work came from critic Aleks Sierz's term *In-Yer-Face Theatre* – a type of drama in the 1990s whose language and imagery were uncompromisingly provocative and violent. While *Closer* does include one brief moment when Dan slaps Alice across the face (2:11.286), it is markedly unlike other work form the period such as Anthony Neilson's *Penetrator* or Sarah Kane's *Cleansed*. And while *Closer* does contain moments of violent and highly emotional language such as the end of scene six where Dan and Anna leave their respective partners, the play does not adopt the experiential approach of 'touching nerves and provoking alarm' that Sierz's sees as indicative of the genre (Sierz 2001: 4). However, this is not to say that *Closer* is any less of an intense or uncomfortable experience, and Marber explains that he set out to produce a play in which formal structure would be in equilibrium with moments of intense emotion:

The idea was to create something that has a formal beauty into which you could shove all this anger and fury. I hoped the dramatic power of the play would rest on that tension between elegant structure – the underlying plan is that you see the first and last meeting of every couple in the play – and inelegant emotion. (Buse 2006)

Closer, with its witty dialogue, and structure based around 'the well-made play', in some ways makes it an odd bedfellow amongst the other in-yer-face dramatists of the late 1990s. Marber has also been is dismissive of his categorization as a 'blood and vomit' playwright, but understands how his inclusion into this category has occurred: '*Closer* had some bad language, so the people make those lists . . . you know, it's just journalism . . . [but] it's better to be talked about than not, nicer to be on the lists than not' (Fray 2003). The decision to cast Kate Ashfield as Liza Walker's replacement for Alice in 1998 during the last months of the play's transfer to the Lyric Theatre perhaps also helped make this association more explicit owing to her appearance in some of the key in-yer-face plays of the period such as Nick Grosso's *Peaches*, Sarah Kane's *Blasted* and Mark Ravenhill's *Shopping and Fucking*.

However, Marber observes that his inclusion into this particular group of dramatists also damaged the reception of his next play *Howard Katz*, especially in terms of obtaining European productions: 'All the German dramaturges who run the theatres are saying, "yeah, we like the play but it's old fashioned and we want plays about child abuse and anal sex and blood and vomit and it ain't that' (Fray 2003). David Ian Rabey, like Marber, observes that 'unlike Kane's *Blasted* or Ravenhill's *Shopping & F***ing*, the shock [of *Closer*] resides in the verbal rather than the visual images', yet he also argues that its intensity is also expressed through the characters' 'uncontrolled, even uncontrollable eloquence [where] the emphasis is not so much on submerged feelings and subtext, as on a fierce, even brutal honesty' (Rabey 2003: 1999).

Such moments obviously render *Closer* problematic when

making a case for it belonging to the genre of comedy. In some respects this *faux* categorization is born out of critical laziness through the obvious assumptions that are made from Marber's background in comedy as well as *Dealer's Choice* winning the Evening Standard Award for Best Comedy in 1995. However, the repeat achievement two years later for *Closer* prompted the critic Michael Robinson to describe it as a 'curious . . . [decision given that] it is sometimes anything but comic' (Robinson 1999: 30). In some respects this was understandable due to moments such as the internet scene which were memorably comic. Peter Buse comments that the humour in *Closer* 'is not a comedy of situation, but of wit and bleak irony', and David Ian Rabey observes that despite being a mordant play *Closer* can still successfully masquerade as a comedy because it 'contains lines and scenes that are in many ways humorous'. However, he adds the important proviso, 'in many ways, but not all ways' (Rabey 2003: 199). Like the characters in the play who appropriate the identities of others, Rabey comments that *Closer* itself 'has the sharp reflecting surface of a comedy with its trick questions and cut-and-thrust repartee . . . But the play invites and draws the imagination beneath surfaces, and identifies potential tragic situations to which the audience might sense their own disturbing proximity and susceptibility' (Rabey 2003: 201). Marber himself also seems to understand the problems critics have encountered in attempting to categorize the play as a comedy:

> It doesn't offend me when people describe it as a comedy. It starts as a romantic comedy with a classic Hollywood cute meet [but] it is a particular kind of dark, bleak *fin de siecle* comedy. (Gardner 1998)

At one point Larry tells Dan, 'you think the human heart is like a diagram' (2:10.272), and in some respects *Closer* is also constructed along similar intricate lines. Peter Buse has described this two act play, with its twelve scenes, divided into six either side of the interval as 'structurally immaculate' (Buse 2006), to the point 'where form and content are in absolute co-existence' (Macaulay 1999). Marber himself has also spoken of the profound influence that 'well-made plays' and 'well-constructed novels' (Sierz 2001: 191–2) have made on his own writing.

Often the comic world is one based on a form of anarchism where the rules that govern everyday conduct are overthrown or subverted. This had been the model Marber and his co-writers adopted on comedy series such as *The Day Today* and *Knowing Me, Knowing You*. However, with *Closer* these anarchic impulses are tightly constrained beneath its formal structure and Marber has commented: 'It was always part of the conception of the play that I would write about big ugly emotions contained within some formally beautiful structure: which makes it crueller' (Shone 1997).

Closer's formal structure is also governed by the use of stage props as well as through its language. Key amongst these is the Newton's Cradle, which we first see on Dan's desk throughout scene three, and which Alice later buys as a present for Larry in scene nine. Marber himself calls this 'sort of the symbol of play – albeit an ironic and tacky one' (Marber 2007: xxv), yet not only does the Newton's Cradle obliquely connect Dan and Larry to Alice as her lovers but as Christopher Innes observes, 'with its swinging metal balls that knock each other out of contact . . . [it] becomes an image of the continually changing pairings in the play' (Innes 2002: 433). Aleks Sierz also points out that the original programme notes to *Closer* include a pertinent quotation from Sir Isaac Newton's famous dictum, 'To every Action there is always opposed an equal reaction'. These 'reactions' constantly reverberate and circulate throughout the play via a whole host of phrases and incidents that produce difficult repercussions for its characters.

The critic Terry Grimley also sees this occurring: 'whenever one character comes to rest in a relationship they transfer their restlessness to their partners' (Grimley 2001). For example, for every 'moment' (2:9.267) when we become consciously aware of falling in love with another person the very opposite reaction of 'I don't love you anymore, goodbye' (1:1.191) co-exists and these polar forces of attraction and repulsion play out constantly between the characters during the course of the play. The operation of these forces were also likened by several critics to choreographic patterns such as 'a mating dance' (Albasani 1997), or a 'a crazy sexual square dance in which partners are constantly swapped' (Spencer 1997), whereby the four characters come together, break apart, swap partners and finally separate – presumably for good.

However, the structure of the play is a good deal more complex than merely being a series of incidents based around cause and effect. *Closer* also employs a structure based on numerous other patterns of circularity, mirroring and repetition. Examples of mirroring range from intimations of Alice's own mortality in the opening scene and its fulfilment in the last, to the opening image of Alice '*pull[ing] out some sandwiches in silver foil*' (1:1.183), and the discovery of their significance at the end. Other examples of mirroring include the two identical Styrofoam cups Dan brings to Alice in the opening scene, to the same cashmere jumper Larry and Alice both wear in the course of the play (1:6.224; 2:9.260). There are also examples of where mirroring is used to accentuate a sense of voyeurism such as the incident in scene five where we see Dan watching Alice, who in turn is looking at '*a huge photograph* of herself' (1:5.213). *Closer* is also full of phrases which are repeated later, often by different characters. Frequently this is done to render a line ironic, or to illustrate a shift in dynamics. For instance, Alice uses the phrase 'we don't want *him* here while we're working, do we' (1:2.201) to suggest first the idea of conspiratorial female solidarity; yet the encounter is manipulated in order to confront Anna that she has overheard Dan's confession of attraction to Anna. Alice later repeats the phrase again to Anna in scene nine – this time in order to persuade her to give up Dan and return to Larry.

Marber has also commented that the structure governing *Closer* is based around the beginnings and endings of relationships:

> The play and the film are constructed around a very simple premise, which is that you see the beginning and the ending of every relationship. That might not be an apparent structure, but that's what it is. I suppose the thinking behind the play was that the beginning and the ending of a relationship are the truly significant events, so I just thought I'd cut the middle out. (Motskin 2004: 34)

As mentioned, one of the plays which *Closer* most resembles in terms of its structure is Harold Pinter's *Betrayal* (1978), where key events are shown backwards through the history of a love triangle; both plays dramatize highly selective moments over time. Adopting such an approach contributes to a sense of dislocation and the possibility of never truly coming to a sense of empathy with the protagonists or an easy understanding of their motivations. However, speaking in relation to *Betrayal* (but applicable to *Closer*), the critic Mark Batty argues that it is this highly selective non-linear narrative approach that gives the audience some parity of engagement between all its characters (Batty 2001: 3).

However, in both plays structure itself ultimately dominates over psychological characterization based on verisimilitude. This is achieved through an approach whereby details of the characters' everyday lives are expunged, while friends and family are relegated to off-stage figures; it is purely the key moments of the central characters' relationships to one another that are of importance. Arguably it is this employment of a dramatic form based on compression and concentration that forces the audience to redirect their responses to the play back on themselves. While Jeremy Kingston found this to be 'oddly unengaging' (Kingston 1997), Tom Shone's account of a woman sobbing through *Closer* is indicative of how it forces the audience to assess themselves when watching the performance (Shone 1997). Shone's account is also similar to Liza Walker's impression when she played Alice, whereby couples after the play become 'really huggy . . . [or] move[d] away from each other' (Sierz 2001: 190).

Just as a formal precision informs structure, this also applies to the use of time. Marber comments about the effect he wished to produce:

> Early on I made the decision that the events of the story were going to occur over four and a half years. And that never changed. I decided that I was going to allow myself time, as opposed to compressing the events into a year, or a month, or writing a play set over a week. I knew it was a story that needed to unfold over time, and once I allowed myself that luxury, the shape was fairly evident to me. (Motskin 2004: 34)

While these gaps are made specific in the text, they are never alluded to in the actual performance, and it is left to the audience to gauge the amount of time that has elapsed between scenes. Larry's observation, '*Time*: what a tricky little fucker' (1:6.227), is also a pertinent comment on other ways in which it is manipulated over the course of the play. For instance, scene six divides the stage into two parallel time schemes in which action moves between two locations as Dan and Anna are about to leave Alice and Larry.

At one point Dan bitterly remarks, 'All the language is old, there are no new words' (1:5.222), yet it is through language that all the relationships in *Closer* are initiated, brokered and finally disintegrate. Marber also produces a highly stylized and economic style of language. Along with an acknowledgement of the influence that fellow dramatists Harold Pinter and David Mamet have exerted on the economy and rhythms of his writing style, Marber also sees his background in stand-up comedy as being educative:

> You learn very quickly to get to the point, and that words are something that get you to the point quickly. In comedy, the more words you have, the more opportunity an audience has to throw things at you. So you learn quickly where the meat of whatever it is that you're saying is. (Macaulay 1999)

This discourse often manifests itself in quick-fire repartee – particularly when characters size each other up with a view to seduction. The following is a typical exchange from the opening scene:

DAN: Didn't fancy my sandwiches?
ALICE: I don't eat fish
DAN: Why not?
ALICE: Fish piss in the sea
DAN: So do children
ALICE: I don't eat children either (1:1.183)

David Ian Rabey also sees this pattern at times developed and 'extended further into three way volleys' (Rabey 2003: 201) such as the following exchange between Dan and Larry:

DAN: (*nods*) I was made editor
LARRY: Yeah? How come?
DAN: The previous editor died (2:11.276)

This brevity of language is most clearly demonstrated in the scene where Dan and Larry communicate via the internet, and where the written language they employ is shortened to facilitate both the speed of normal spoken conversation together with the maximum erotic charge possible:

DAN: I want 2 suck U senseless
LARRY: B my guest
DAN: Sit on my face Fuckboy
LARRY: I'm there
DAN: Wear my wet knickers
Beat
LARRY: ok
DAN: RU well hung?
LARRY: 9£

Like the use of language in Pinter and Mamet, at first the exchanges between Marber's characters seem to be an attempt to approximate the language and rhythms of everyday speech, yet in fact are highly stylized in their construction. Marber, if anything, is even more punctilious in the care and precision afforded to the implicit meaning of individual words and phrases. In this way he leaves little to chance by almost coaching the actual delivery of lines to the would be actor. This is achieved in large part through his practice of italicizing or underlining particular words and phrases, to where in moments of extreme emotion block capitals are used. The following exchange between Anna and Larry at the Aquarium in scene four, where the latter discovers he has been tricked by Dan on the internet, demonstrates all three methods in action:

LARRY: What a PRICK. He's <u>advertising</u>! *Why?* Why would he
             pretend to be you?
ANNA: He likes me (1:4.211)

While adopting such a methodology could be seen as imposing an overt authorial presence that could be seen as restrictive, marking out the text in such a distinctive way highlights the pace and rhythms which govern its structure and are in turn intrinsic to its meaning.

Gender and relationships

Shortly after *Closer* opened at the Royal National Theatre, Patrick Marber was asked about the motivation behind its writing:

> One of the starting points for the play was that I hadn't, since the film *Sex, Lies and Videotape*, seen anything that put my generations' romantic concerns in any kind of perspective. Soap does that to some extent, but soap is about working class people and my plays are about middle- to lower-middle-class people. (Shone 1997)

Marber's reference to Stephen Soderbergh's film *Sex, Lies and Videotape* articulated similar concerns facing heterosexual relationships during the 1980s, where established patterns of conduct had either radically changed or been called into question. Soderbergh's film explores adultery between a husband with his wife's sister, and like *Closer* is both emotionally charged, yet also distanced through the character of Graham who records on video female acquaintances discussing intimate details of their sex lives.

Marber's comment about not finding a contemporary work that expressed his generation's views about relationships were articulated by the television drama series *This Life* (1996–7), which came out just prior to *Closer*. Its creator Amy Jenkins, makes a very similar comment to Marber: 'I wanted to give a voice to my generation . . . There's a new cynicism – or reality – about relationships because so many of us have seen our parents split up' (www.televisionheaven.co.uk). Marber's recognition that soap-opera only partly expressed modern concerns also became the basis of *This Life,* whose characters were also largely drawn from the professional classes.

Closer was praised for both its emotional honesty, which erupted at certain moments from beneath its witty dispassionate surface. As has been mentioned, *Closer* has been compared to Harold Pinter's *Betrayal*; however, it was these moments of stark brutality that distinguished *Closer* from Pinter's play about adultery – where ultimately Robert's long-standing friendship with Jerry merits far more importance than knowledge of his affair with Robert's wife. Whereas the critic Mark Batty observes that in *Betrayal* 'infidelity [is] pretty much the sexual status quo' (Batty 2001: 70, 72), and a gentlemanly accommodation can be arranged – this is markedly absent in *Closer*. The actress Julia Roberts, who was later to star in the film version, gives a good account of the painful emotional rawness to *Closer* when she went to see the production in London:

> I didn't like it, not because it wasn't good but because it was just so ugly to me. In London theatres they serve ice-cream at the concession stands, and I remember standing up when the play was over and seeing all these ice-cream wrappers on the floor and thinking 'ice-cream? What we need are martinis and razor blades'. (Smith 2004)

Overall *Closer* adopts a bleak sensibility to human relationships. Christopher Innes observes that that the play depicts 'a society where sex has become commodified and true feeling impossible . . . [where] the characters are depicted as almost hermetically sealed off from the world around them' (Innes 2002: 431). Marber himself has compared *Closer* to 'love as a poker game . . . [and] the dynamic of power' (www.newyorkmetro.com), and perhaps one of its most telling speeches – and one which also reveals its pessimistic nature is Alice's response to Dan when he pleads with her not to leave:

Show me. Where is this '*love*'?
I can't see it, I can't *touch* it, I can't *feel* it
I can <u>hear</u> it, I can hear some <u>words</u> but I can't *do* anything with
your easy words (2:11.285)

While we see the romance of initial attraction between Dan/Alice
(1.1), Dan/Anna (1.2), Anna/Larry (1.5) and Alice/Larry (1.5) that
is spontaneous and unexplained, love itself seems absent in the
world of play. As mentioned, Alice is the character most aware of its
possibilities, but also its elusiveness. When Dan in the opening
scene asks what Alice wants from life she replies, 'To be loved', and
although Dan's rejoinder is, 'That simple', Alice recognizes that 'It's
a big want' (1:1.192). While the other characters often delude
themselves that they are in love, Alice again remains most aware of
the true situation. For instance, in the final confrontation Anna's
defence that adultery was beyond her control is fiercely interro-
gated by Alice:

'I fell in love' – as if you had no *choice*.
There's a moment, there's always a *moment*; I can do this, I can
give in to this or I can resist it . . . You didn't fall in love, you gave
in to temptation (2.9.267)

In the same scene Alice nonchalantly reveals that with Dan, 'I
didn't *fall* in love. I chose to' (2:9.267), a seemingly arbitrary
decision taken immediately after noticing his crustless sandwiches
on their first meeting at the hospital. David Ian Rabey also
observes an alternative process taking place in the relationships
that define *Closer*, based around mutual attraction rather than
love:

It suggests that it is indefinite possibility, rather than definite
qualities, which attract, compulsively; that this attraction sparks

the appetite for the sexually definite, compulsively; and that discovery of the definite ultimately separates people, compulsively.
(Rabey 2003: 201)

This reading seems to equate human attraction to a set of discrete
sexual forces that act upon the characters rather than ascribing
these to the mysterious fluctuations that govern romantic love.
This is a convincing reading, when amongst the brutality and
chaos that falling in love costs, Marber deliberately includes motifs
borrowed from the medieval tradition of Courtly Love. This if
anything only succeeds in accentuating competitive and painful
feelings at the expense of the romantic. These courtly references are
numerous: for example, Dan and Alice address each other as, 'You
knight/You *damsel* (1:1.185) in the opening scene, and Dan also
uses the same practice in his virtual 'wooing' of Larry on the
internet; after a conversation couched in the crude language of
male pornographic fantasy Dan ends the conversation by writing,
'I send U a Rose my love . . .' followed by an illustration made out
of figures from his computer keyboard (1:4.208).

As has been mentioned, elements from the genre of Restoration
Comedy can be detected in *Closer*, notably the theme of male
cuckoldry. While it was still playing at the Royal National Theatre,
in February 1998 Terry Johnson's adaptation of Edward Raven-
scroft's *The London Cuckolds* opened at the Lyttleton, and audiences could make direct comparisons between male rivalry being
played out for comic effect, against the Darwinian struggle in
Closer. The sexual rivalry between Dan and Larry revisits the
familiar Restoration idea of the 'biter bit', where Larry gains his
revenge on Dan (who had originally tricked Larry with his internet
'disguise' as Anna and then later cuckolds him with the real Anna),
by persuading Anna to sleep with him one last time. Marber also
manages to reverse what critic J. Douglas Canfield observes to be
the class based obsessions in Restoration Comedy, where lower

class characters are, 'no match for the perfect bodies and wits of the class designed by nature to rule, who have the right of the *seigeur* sexually to dominate their inferiors' (Owen 2001: 214). As mentioned, Larry seems to cast himself as socially inferior to others and in a brief truce during their climactic scene, the pair discuss their respective father's occupations: the difference between the two – Larry's father is a taxi-driver and Dan's was a teacher – accentuates the class differences between the two men. However, despite his background Larry emerges as victorious and the scene ends with Larry disclosing that he has twice cuckolded Dan by proxy through an affair with his ex-partner Alice.

Although Richard Eyre believes that *Closer* is more concerned in exploring sex rather than sexual politics (Marber 2004: xii), like Marber's engagement with Strindberg in *After Miss Julie*, human relationships in both plays are shown as Darwinian struggles for power. As mentioned, this is most obvious during scene seven at the lap dancing club, but Marber also shows it to be operating just as fiercely between Anna and Alice in scene nine. For instance, when Alice attempts to persuade Anna to give up Dan the encounter becomes a battle for the survival of the fittest:

ANNA:　It's not a competition
ALICE:　Yes it is
ANNA:　I don't want a fight
ALICE:　SO GIVE IN (2:9.266)

Closer also identifies and exposes a further trait of masculine behaviour: namely an obsessive need to know the truth about a partner's sexual infidelities. However, even when this is disclosed – such as Anna's confession of adultery on two different occasions between Dan and Larry – the effect is never cathartic. The newspaper critic Paul Taylor believes that this obsession to know the truth is disingenuous and stems from a 'bullying, sadomasochistic need to know the anatomical facts . . . about their partner's infidelities' (Taylor 1997). In this light, Anna's comment about '[taking it] Like a _man_' (2:9.264) is meant ironically; instead of the stoic reception that the phrase implies, in _Closer_ the men are deeply wounded by female rejection. David Ian Rabey observes that this male 'insistence upon honesty and explicitness tends to inflame their jealously' (Rabey 2003: 199), while Neil Norman saw this as part of a masculine trait rooted in 'the masochistic need to feel the pain of the betrayal in the details' – while at the same time using it as a way of attacking their erstwhile partners by being able to 'act as the wounded party and recapture the higher moral ground' (Chunn and Norman 1998).

Allied to this Darwinian struggle is an equally bleak outlook on the gulf of mutual understanding between men and women. During a brief moment of truce with Alice, Anna observes that men judge their relationships with women in the following way: 'They spend a lifetime fucking and never know how to make love . . . They love the way we make them _feel_ but not "us"' (2:10.268).

The last scene of the play also becomes a coda – not only for Dan, Larry and Anna to mourn the death of Alice – but for love itself. As David Ian Rabey observes, 'by the end of the play, the characters are less "closer" than ever before, deliberately flouting romantic hopes [for the audience] (Rabey 2003: 199). This desolate ending is underscored by Dan's account of a chance meeting between his ex-lover Ruth who in the interim has married and had children with a Spanish poet after translating a collection of his poems entitled _Solitude_ (2:12.292). By the end of the play it seems the remaining characters are moving inexorably towards the same fate: Dan seems to have found no one to replace Alice since her death, Anna has bought a dog and retreated to the countryside to live alone, and while Larry is now with a nurse called Polly, who he confides to Anna is not 'the one' (2:12.287–8).

The cityscape

The cover of Patrick Marber's *Plays: 1* shows a photo-montage by the Austrian Bauhaus artist Herbert Beyer of a pair of hands spread out against the façade of city buildings, over which a pair of eyes are superimposed on the palms of the hands. The photograph, entitled 'Lonely Metropolitan' (www.methuen.co.uk/marberplays1.html) is an apt image for Marber's work: as Peter Buse observes, with the notable exception of *After Miss Julie*, *Dealer's Choice*, *Closer* and *Howard Katz*, all form a 'loose trilogy of plays in and about contemporary London' (Buse 2006). The 2007 production of *Don Juan* in Soho could also justifiably claim to make up a quartet.

The location is not coincidental. From *Dealer's Choice* onwards the relationship of the individual to their urban environment has been a crucial theme in his work. In the quote below Marber talks about the importance of London in *Closer*:

> It is almost all set within a mile of where I live in Smithfield. I used to walk my dog in Postman's Park, where the Watt's Memorial of Heroic Deeds is situated. I was also much influenced by Milan Kundera and the idea of the city as a place of coincidence and strangeness, a place where people aren't organically connected. There is also a lot of Jonathan Raban's *Soft City* in it. (Gardner 1998)

The centrality of London also preoccupied Marber's *Howard Katz* and *Don Juan in Soho*, although an offhand comment given just prior to the Broadway opening of *Closer* in 1999 seemed to indicate that Marber's next play was going to be a modern version of Jacobean City Comedy: 'What I want to write is a great big funny play, a huge bitter vicious laughter machine, a big Jonsonian public play' (Macaulay 1999).

While *Closer* bears very little direct comparison to plays such as Ben Jonson's *The Alchemist* (1610) or *Bartholomew Fair* (1614), nevertheless ideas and motifs from this particular genre can be detected: both attach great importance not only to specific locations, but the geographical and social demarcations these imply as well as the connection between character and location – such as the opening descriptions given to Dan, Larry, Alice and Anna (182). While Christopher Innes sees this as indicative of the characters' backgrounds 'cover[ing] the whole of English society' (Innes 2002: 431), Marber's intentions seem to be more concerned with the characters' relationship to the metropolis itself.

Closer is also concerned with specific London locations. The theatre programme for its transfer to the Lyric Theatre in 1998 includes photographs of the principal London landmarks featured in the play: Saint Bartholomew's Hospital, Blackfriars Bridge, Smithfield's Meat Market and the Aquarium at London Zoo.

However, the contemporary London cityscape at times feels as if it is merely a temporary structure, a palimpsest to older versions of itself. For instance, in scene two we learn of the 'buried river' (1:2.194) known as the Fleet that runs below Anna's studio and which had been built over during the eighteenth century. However, the period from London's past which most dominates *Closer* is Victorian. Richard Eyre mentions that the follow up to *Dealer's Choice* was originally going to be a play about a reading group that meet at a flat in an affluent part of London to discuss George Eliot's novel *Middlemarch* (1871–2); a car alarm alerts them to a robbery taking place by a gang of black youths which culminates in a citizens arrest and one of the boys being brought back to the flat. (Marber 2004: xi). This not only seems to suggest that Victorian culture was an ongoing interest but also its juxtaposition and continued influence on contemporary London.

The ending of *Closer* certainly has affinities with literature from the period, in which both the plot and principal themes of the play revolve around the G. F. Watts Memorial at Postman's Park. Larry's dismissal of the monument as 'the sentimental act of a Victorian philanthropist' (2:12.290) is echoed by Dominic Dromgoole's view of the Victorian influences on *Closer* as 'Dickensian *faux-naïf*' (Dromgoole 2000: 195). Nevertheless, the 1998 theatre programme contained an explanatory note about the Victorian painter G. F. Watts and his memorial in Postman's park, commemorating acts of heroism by ordinary people. Marber has also spoken about the function and importance of this specific location:

> The Watts Memorial connected to incoherent ideas that I was wanting to explore, which had to do with the kindness of strangers and the romantic idea that somewhere in the world is the person who we will immediately connect with and spend the rest of our lives with. But I've limited the information about Watts to a minimum because I could feel the audience saying 'Why are we getting a history lesson?' (www.ramagazine.org.uk)

Watts' brief first marriage to the 16-year-old Ellen Terry (Watts was 47) prompted by a misguided belief on Watts' part that he was somehow rescuing her from the shame of having to act on the stage, parallels Dan and Larry's attitude to Alice in wanting to rescue her from stripping. However, Postman's Park is important to *Closer* in a number of other ways: for instance, we learn that the name of Alice Ayres has been appropriated from one of the memorial plaques by the person calling herself 'Alice'. The park is also the location that binds its other three principal characters together. Dan remembers it as the place where he learnt the news of his mother's death (1:1.187); Larry uses it as a place to smoke surreptitiously (1:5.218) and it finally becomes the gathering place where the three remaining characters temporarily reunite after Alice's death.

Another cityscape also exerts a strong presence on the London of *Closer* – that of New York. Alice has just returned from there in the opening scene, and it is the destination that Alice and Dan were about to visit before breaking up for the last time: it is also the place where Alice meets her death. New York seems to hold a particular significance for Marber; in *After Miss Julie*, rather than using Strindberg's original choice of Italy's Lake Como, New York becomes the destination for John and Julie's escape from the postwar austerity of England: 'New York. That's the place for us. Yeah? New life, new people . . . They love us over there, they die for the accent' (152). In *Closer*, while the city is still depicted as glamorous, it is also tinged with a seedy decadence. Larry's description, 'what a town: it's a twenty-four-hour pageant called "Whatever You Want"' (1:6.228), presages his confession to Anna about visiting a prostitute while staying in the city. New York and American culture in general also make its influence felt on the London cityscape. For instance, Larry is unable to recognize the punk club of his youth now that it has been transformed into the type of lap dancing club he visited in New York and Alice sardonically observes while she is stripping, 'England always imports the best of America' (2:7.241).

3 Production History

Closer: The Play

This chapter is a brief history of significant productions of *Closer* as well as the film version of the play.

Closer originally started out as a commission from the Royal National Theatre, prompted by the success of *Dealer's Choice*. Marber began working on the play in the summer of 1996, but the original conception of a satirical modern city comedy shifted, owing to personal circumstances:

> A bit of life happened to me. Romantic stuff, a series of events in my personal life. I had been beginning to think of writing a play and I thought this is good stuff and I can use it. (Gardner 1998)

The first draft was completed relatively quickly by November, although Marber was late in coming up with a title:

> The reason I eventually decided to call it *Closer* rather than say, *Love, Sex and Other Miseries* was that I didn't want to close down the options for the audience about what it was about. For me, it was about identity, the city, death and the need to do something before you die. And the fact that the self who falls in and out of love may be a very different person from the one who walks the dog, goes to work and makes the tea. (Gardner 1998)

Following the same pattern as *Dealer's Choice*, the new play underwent a two week series of workshops at the National Theatre Studio
during December. *Closer* had also undergone an earlier workshop in
September where the actors Anna Chancellor, Douglas Hodge,
Jason Isaacs and Claire Skinner performed early scenes as work-in-
progress. The December workshop also employed another group of
well known actors – Kate Beckinsale, Sally Dexter, Stephen Dillane
and Mark Strong – and culminated in a reading of the play before an
invited audience. Dexter and Strong both recall the process of the
workshops:

> I ended up . . . working on this play the size of a telephone direc-
> tory. We'd rehearse it voicing objections, making comments,
> trying things out, and Patrick would come back each day with
> changes and new scenes.

> I was totally intrigued by it [*Closer*] and Patrick's way of working.
> He seems to need the actors to visualize the characters. I always
> wondered how the thing was going to stand up when it got to
> production, because it's a bunch of four people reacting quite
> cerebrally. There are no obvious theatrical fireworks. It's very
> lean. (Gardner 1998)

Both accounts seem to suggest a high degree of involvement and
Marber has commented, 'At least a third of *Closer* was rewritten in
rehearsals because of what the actors brought to it' (Sierz 2001:
191). This process of ongoing revision subsequently became a
feature of *Closer*, where changes in cast and theatre venue provided
Marber with opportunities to make further cuts and changes; this
progress can be charted in the three revised editions of the play
from 1997 to 2004.

In a pattern that has established itself from *Dealer's Choice*
through to *Howard Katz*, Patrick Marber has directed the first

British productions of his own work. With *Closer* Marber discovered an important facet to his work – namely that for him at least, the process of writing and directing were indistinguishable from each other as working methods:

> Sam Mendes was going to direct it, but as the first day of rehearsals drew nearer there was still no finished play. Also, he [Mendes] was going to have to do it back to back with *Antony and Cleopatra* and the Donmar [Warehouse] was having problems at the time. So he pulled out, which was how I came to direct it, which was probably just as well because as soon as I'd written the first draft I realized that my working method is to write, cut and re-draft all the way through rehearsal. I even change it now. When you stop changing things, it's dead. (Gardner 1998)

Closer opened at the Royal National Theatre's Cottesloe auditorium on 22 May 1997 with a cast of Liza Walker as Alice, Clive Owen as Dan, Ciaran Hinds as Larry and Sally Dexter as Anna. Dexter was the only member of the original actors from the original National Studio workshops to be cast in the first production, although Mark Strong knew he would be unable to appear due to a prior commitment in a touring production of Arthur Miller's *Death of a Salesman*. However, he was to join the cast of *Closer* when it transferred to the Lyttleton. One advantage of the workshop sessions prior to formal rehearsals was that it allowed Marber to reshape material for a specific actor. In this case, Marber recognized that the role of Anna was directly influenced by the work Sally Dexter had already undertaken in the workshops:

> Casting the play is like running a dating agency . . . Because Sally had been Anna in the workshops in the later drafts she was the face and voice of the character. I wrote for her. But with the

others it was more difficult. Things which seem incredibly important when you are writing become less important when you're casting it. (Gardner 1998)

While Dexter, Hinds and Owen were relatively well known names, Liza Walker was a newcomer and *Closer* her first professional work for theatre. She recalls her surprise at being contacted for the part:

I don't know how Patrick found me. I wasn't even in Spotlight [the actor's directory]. I just got a 'phone call saying, go and collect a script from the National Theatre . . . I went to read it for Patrick the next day, and the day after that I heard I'd got the part. Patrick was taking an enormous risk because I'd never been on stage before. (Gardner 1998)

The 300-seat Cottesloe is the smallest of the three principal stages at the National Theatre, but after a successful residency the play transferred to the larger 890-seat Lyttleton Theatre on 16 October 1997. Both Marber and the cast were struck at the time on how both the play in performance and its audience's reactions changed with the move to a larger venue. Marber described the intimacy of the Cottlesloe with its audience adjacent to the performers as 'snarling' (Marber 1998b), and Mark Strong as 'brutal': in contrast, the Lyttleton space tended to accentuate the more formal or 'lyrical' (Marber 1998b). Marber commented that the move accentuated other features of *Closer* – namely its language rhythms and intricate formal structure. Mark Strong also observed that audiences were more 'dispassionate and distanced' (Forrest 1997), which paradoxically made them more responsive to the humour of the play.

The designer chosen for *Closer* was Vicki Mortimer, who had collaborated previously with Marber on his adaptation of Craig

Raine's *'1953'*. Her initial reading of the play identified the tightly knit structure of the text as well as the symbolic importance London exerts on its characters. This observation led Mortimer to introduce a device whereby the stage saw a steady accumulation of props, which were left to build up rather than being taken away between scenes:

> I wanted to give it a London root, but most of all I felt it was crucial in the staging to make it clear that there are echoes beyond the given consequences of any scene. So, for example, though there is furniture it's not naturalistic, and the way it is moved to the back of the stage and stays there throughout makes it clear that everyone's regrets, words and actions remain – they are always there. (Gardner 1998)

Mortimer's design was notable for its minimalism which contributed to the bleaker mood of the play. In contrast, critic Michael Raab gives a humorous account of *Closer*'s German debut at the Munich Kammerspiele in Autumn 1997, which was dominated by an intrusive 'conceptual' set design in which 'huge towers covered with ugly black rubber were lugged around by a small army of stage-hands without making a significant difference when the curtain opened again' (Raab 2002: 141–2).

The German production also ignored the specific London settings that Mortimer evoked through a design that incorporated a permanent backdrop consisting of a series of large ceramic plaques that represented the actual memorials in Postman's Park. Sound designer Simon Baker also recalls the London setting influencing the use of music for its original British production:

> It was a question of setting Paddy's [Cunneen] music within the London landscape of the play. I went for a generic and quite aggressive sound – lots of taxi brakes, which I think for most

people are really the sound of London. I melded that with Paddy's strings. It gives quite a hardcore edge, a sense of the anonymous city. (Gardner 1998)

Originally Marber was not going to use live music in *Closer*, and its composer Paddy Cuneen only produced the original score relatively late into rehearsals:

Patrick told me he was doing a modern love story. Originally we decided that it didn't need composed music but popular reference points. Then Patrick was keen to have something more romantic. He felt it needed emotional drive. I think we were talking Elvis Costello. Then about two weeks into rehearsal I realized I really wanted to compose the music myself. Watching it in rehearsal, I began to realize the play was fundamentally about passion. My original idea was to do it using a soprano sax, which is moody and melancholic, but has a spiky energy too. But Patrick was insistent it should be a cello. (Gardner 1998)

From the Lyttleton *Closer* moved to the Lyric Theatre in London's West End on 19 March 1998. Speaking at the time, Marber felt that the new location would perfectly suit the play's blend of carefully constructed language and emotional intensity: 'It's an intimate house so the play's brutality is uncompromised but the proscenium arch will, I hope give the production a little poetry too' (Marber 1998b).

The lengthy ten month residency at the Royal National Theatre had seen the replacement of its two principal male roles: Mark Strong replaced Clive Owen as Dan and Neil Dudgeon replaced Ciaran Hinds as Larry. Now, the move to the Lyric also saw further significant cast changes: Frances Barber replaced Sally Dexter as Anna, while Lloyd Owen and Neil Pearson were cast as Dan and Larry respectively – only Liza Walker now remained from the original cast.

With the changes in casting, Marber also took the opportunity to make minor textual revisions to the play. In interview, he discussed both the nature of these changes and the rationale behind them:

They're fairly small changes (in general) but the intention is usually to focus the narrative line. Every time I go back into rehearsals with a new cast new ideas seem to occur. This seems to me to be entirely healthy. The more I direct the play the more I understand it. It's still a new play and it's a living text which can always be improved. (Marber 1998b)

Closer ran at the Lyric for eight months, finally closing on 31 October 1998. During this time further cast changes took place. Liza Walker finally left the production and was replaced by Kate Ashfield in the role of Alice, while Imogen Stubbs replaced Frances Barber as Anna and Tom Mannion replaced Neil Pearson as Larry. Lloyd Owen stayed on in the role of Dan.

In interview, Kate Ashfield recalls the difficulties of being called upon to replace Liza Walker who had originally created the role of Alice:

Before I auditioned, Patrick Marber asked me to see the production and I saw Liza Walker play Alice. She'd trained as a dancer so has a real elegance that I don't possess at all. What Liza naturally brought to the part of Alice was that grace and capacity for other people to want to look after her; and I couldn't really capture that. What you can do is bring other things to the role. It's very hard to take over from someone else so I felt I was pretty dreadful during rehearsals. If I knew that Liza Walker had done something during rehearsals then I would purposefully not do it! (Saunders 2002)

The critical and commercial success of the first British production of *Closer* was demonstrated through the series of accolades it received during 1997: these included the Critics Circle and Laurence Oliver/BBC Awards for Best New Play, the Evening Standard Award for Best Comedy and Time Out Award for Best West End Play.

With such indicators of success in London, it is perhaps of little surprise that the play would attract the attention of Broadway, and on 25 March 1999 *Closer* opened at the Music Box Theatre in New York. In some respects the way had already been paved by the opening of David Hare's play *The Blue Room* at the Court Theatre in December 1998, and which closed one month before *Closer* premiered. *The Blue Room* was a loose adaptation of Arthur Schitznler's play *Reigen* (1900) – but more popularly known as *La Ronde*. Although Hare's play received decidedly mixed critical reviews it became a media event in New York for much the same reason during its London debut – namely a brief nude scene involving the celebrated Hollywood actress Nicole Kidman. While *Closer* contained no nudity, it did share certain thematic similarities with *The Blue Room*: these included the almost geometric swapping of partners and the bleak as well as destructive power that can accompany sexual desire. This, together with the publicity generated from Hare's play as well as the reputation from its London production, generated a certain degree of anticipation for *Closer*'s Broadway opening.

The production was again directed by Marber, with a cast that included Ciaran Hinds as Dan from the original Cottesloe production (although on that occasion he played the role of Larry), Rupert Graves as Dan and Natasha Richardson as Anna. Like Liza Walker, a relative newcomer – Anna Friel – was cast as Alice. Although almost completely unknown to New York audiences, Friel was familiar in Britain, principally from her role as Beth Jordache in the soap-opera *Brookside* (1982–2003), in which she attracted tabloid notoriety after her character exchanged a same-sex kiss. The presence of Friel made the Broadway production a newsworthy item in the British press, but she also attracted the attention of several New York critics who singled her out for special merit, describing her performance as 'burst[ing] over the Broadway sky like a bombshell' (Lyons 1999) and 'the most appealing new face on Broadway this season' (Zoglin 1999).

Closer also won widespread praise from the New York critics, who described it as, 'a smart, sexy and sublimely funny play' (Lyons 1999) and '*Closer* does not merely hold your attention; it burrows into you' (Simon 1999). The production was also a popular success, and enjoyed a five-month run ending in September, during which it won the New York Critics Award for Best Foreign Play.

In late December 1999 *Closer* made a brief and unexpected return to the Royal National Theatre's Lyttleton stage for thirteen performances in a new production after the sudden closure of Stephen Poliakoff's troubled production of *Remember This*. However this production of *Closer* was not directed by Patrick Marber, but Paddy Cunneen, who had written its musical score. Unlike previous casts, the actors – Amanda Ryan (Alice), Barnaby Kay (Dan), Darrell D'Silva (Larry) and Lizzy McInnery (Anna) – were not 'star' names and before unexpectedly occupying the Royal National Theatre's schedule had been on national/international tour with the play since September, visiting locations as disparate as the Mussovet Theatre in Moscow and Poole Arts Centre, Dorset.

The next major British revival of *Closer* was in 2001 with a production at the 850-seat Birmingham Repertory Theatre. The production was notable for several reasons: not only was it the first production to be directed by Jonathan Church, who had just taken over as the theatre's Artisitc Director but, as mentioned earlier, it was performed in repertory with a production of Noel Coward's *Private Lives*. At the time of writing this has been the only major

British revival of the play since 1997. However in 2004 – seven years after its debut at the Royal National Theatre – and with a production budget of 27 million dollars, *Closer* underwent adaptation into a very different medium.

Closer: The Film

The worldwide theatrical success of *Closer* meant that from relatively early on Marber had received offers to make a film version of the play; yet he had been wary of doing so for a number of factors. Chief amongst these concerned his own intimate and long-standing involvement in the play as its director, and it wasn't until the Broadway production had closed in 1999 that Marber seriously considered some of the film offers:

> I just wanted to sell it to the right person. I was really waiting for a filmmaker to approach me. Producers and various actors had tried to buy the rights over the years, but I really wanted to wait until someone approached me. (Hennigan, see 'Websites' in Further Reading section)

One of the notable early figures who expressed an interest had been the director Mike Nichols. He had established a long and impressive career in Hollywood with credits to his name including *The Graduate* (1967), *Carnal Knowledge* (1971) and *Silkwood* (1983). However, what initially attracted Marber to Nichols was his track record in directing films that had originally been written for the stage:

> He's very experienced at taking a play and turning it into a film, as he'd done with [Edward Albee's] *Who's Afraid of Virginia Woolf?*, and more recently with [Margaret Edson's] *Wit* and [Tony Kushner's] *Angels in America*. And he came from a theatre

background, so I knew he would understand the weirdness of being a playwright and having your play turned into something else. (Hennigan, see 'Websites' in Further Reading section)

Unlike the London and New York theatre productions Marber chose not to direct the film himself, although in their early conversations Nichols gave him the option:

Mike was offering his services as a potential director, or a potential producer, or a collaborator, in some form. He was just into the material.

He was offering a blank canvas of possibilities. (Motskin 2004)

While in the end Marber chose not to direct, he did undertake the task of adapting *Closer* for the screen. As a writer this presented unique challenges, including the temptation to explicate or add to existing material. The play is noteworthy in that its four principal characters very much exist in isolation; and while family, work colleagues and ex-partners are mentioned, none of them actually appear. Marber originally wanted to include some of these off-stage characters in the film but was discouraged by Mike Nichols: 'He said, "Absolutely not. I don't want to see these people"' (Seguin 2004) and the film's only other speaking parts are brief exchanges from a taxi driver and a passport officer. In another interview Marber expands on Nichols decision to keep *Closer*'s theatrical origins highly visible in the film version:

Mike was very clear from the very beginning that he wanted to follow the same structure as the play. He wanted to make a film with a series of long sequences. He didn't want itty bitty scenes and for me to really open it out and invent other characters. He wanted it to be as intense as the play had been. So a ground rule was always we're only going to have four speaking parts in this film. And because he was so clear about that, the process was more really, about cutting and rewriting and making scenes happen in a few more locations than they do in the play. But [adapting] was really all about the dialogue, rather than the shape. (Motskin 2004)

This also meant that the refusal to alert audiences over changes in time between scenes was retained in the film, although it would have been a relatively simple matter to use the familiar cinematic grammar of screen titles to indicate scene changes.

However, the decision to keep to the theatrical structure of the original was not always adhered too, especially on occasions when the technology of cinema could successfully approximate theatrical conditions. A case in point is scene six of the play where the stage is divided in half as we witness the two couples breaking up almost simultaneously: while a cinematic equivalence for this effect could be achieved relatively easily by splitting the screen to show the two scenes together, this was rejected in favour of filming the two scenes separately and editing them as back to back sequences. Also, certain cinematic properties were used to complement elements of the theatrical production that could never have been fully realized owing to limitations of the medium. For instance, in the scene where Larry encounters Alice working at the lap dancing club the audience have to imagine the 'cameras in the ceiling' (2:7.244), but the film allows us to view the pair briefly from the perspective of the hidden cameras situated above.

The film version also exploited an idea only ever partly realized in the play. During the lap dancing scene Alice tells Larry that they can be observed via a two-way mirror (2:7.245), which in the theatre becomes the space occupied by the audience – the so-called 'fourth wall': the film develops this idea of observation through mirrors as a recurrent motif. At one point in the play Larry reports that the mirror in his bathroom seems to goad him by saying, 'Who the fuck are you?' (1:6.228), and the film plays with this uncertainty of human identity presented by reflecting surfaces. For example, Larry is momentarily fooled at the Aquarium when he mistakes Anna's reflected image in front of him as the real person; similarly, Alice checks her reflection in the bathroom mirror immediately after being reassured by Dan that he is not going to leave her: however, it is in the environment of the lap dancing club where the motif is most fully explored. Mark Raggett, who supervised art direction on the film recalls the design of this particular scene, where the juxtaposition between the persona of Alice Ayres the stripper and Jane Jones the person is suggested through the set, which he describes as 'this surreal environment with a staircase of mirrors and translucent walls . . . [which] perfectly captures the reflective mood of this scene' (www.sonypictures.com/movies/closer).

In turn, Dan uses reflecting surfaces at two pivotal moments as confirmation of decisions he has taken and as a method of self-scrutiny: one involves seeing himself in the toilet mirror after he realizes Anna has slept with her estranged husband Larry, and the other is when he catches sight of himself in the airport hotel lift before going back to confront Alice about her brief affair with Larry. Again, one could argue that these sequences are used as cinematic equivalents for the ways that shifting identities in the play are often communicated through verbal exchanges.

The theatricality of the film version led to criticism in some quarters. One review described it as 'a hunk of stagy jaw-jaw' (Sandhu 2005), although this perhaps misses the intention of the film, which attempted to capture as far as possible the mood and rhythms of the play, which were mainly established through the verbal interaction of the actors.

At the same time the film version is far from being a verbatim recording of the play; with a running time of approximately

98 minutes the film is considerably shorter than the play which lasts – based on running times from theatre programmes of the London productions – approximately two and a half hours. Also, with about 30 per cent of the original lines of the play removed, the film is notable for what it *excludes* than includes. For example, Marber removed dialogue that he felt belonged more comfortably onstage and even deleted scene nine where Alice and Anna confront each other for a second time. In the play this is an important scene as it shows Alice fighting Anna for possession of Dan. However, Marber observed that the economy of cinema – 'with one close-up you have the sense of who she is and what's happened' (Seguin 2004) – made the scene redundant.

Marber also decided to include more London locations to the film. While adding a sense of realism to *Closer*, it also diminishes a sense of theatricality. This was most apparent in the equivalent of scene eight, where Anna/Larry and Anna/Dan meet at the same restaurant; in the theatre, midway through the timescale changes simply through Dan occupying the seat vacated by Larry. However, in the film, this separation is achieved by a change of location where Anna first meets Larry at the restaurant in the National Portrait Gallery, and then later at Theatre Royal, Drury Lane, where she meets Dan. In between, we briefly see Anna and Larry dressing after sex in Larry's new consulting room.

Similarly, Alice's speeches about Smithfield's Meat Market and Postman's Park in scene one, together with the symbolism associated with these locations, are cut in the film: instead a short additional scene was inserted near the opening, where Dan and Alice after their meeting at the hospital briefly visit both Postman's Park, together with a whole host of other well-known London landmarks. This scene, together with the casting of the American actress Natalie Portman makes the character of Alice somewhat different from her theatrical incarnation, who is far more intimately and symbolically bound to London.

At the same time the film is able to depict the city of New York physically, such as the last scene which shows Alice's return, whereas in the play New York only ever existed in discussions between characters. Its overt presence in the film was accentuated by the casting of its two American actresses – Natalie Portman as Alice and Julia Roberts as Anna. With its fifty-fifty Anglo-American split (with Jude Law as Dan and Clive Owen as Larry), the film also made explicit what were the more allusive comparisons in the play between London and New York.

Perhaps the most significant change that Marber brought to the film was its conclusion. To say that it ended happily is perhaps an exaggeration, but Alice's death in the play is excluded and the film ends with her back in New York. The final scene from the play set in Postman's Park where Anna, Larry and Dan meet, now bound only by news of Alice's death, is also cut and instead we see Larry and Anna back together again and sharing a bed – although the fact that Larry is sleeping and Anna is still awake implies that the relationship might not be all it seems.

Unlike the London and New York theatre productions which cast together familiar and unknown actors, the film version was notable for its high profile Anglo-American cast. The reasons for this are not hard to see: generally a film aims to appeal to a mass worldwide audience, whereas *Closer* in its many stage productions was usually translated into the language of that country and cast with indigenous actors.

Most well known from the film cast was Julia Roberts, although she was not the first choice to play Anna. Originally the Australian actress Cate Blanchett was to play the role, but she had fallen pregnant before the film was ready for shooting and had to withdraw in September 2003. The other members of the cast were drawn from the ranks of rising new names in the film industry.

Clive Owen was the only cast member who had been directly involved in the play, appearing in the original Cottesloe production as Dan. However, in the film he took on the role of Larry, and Marber commented after the film had been completed that, 'he had the soul of Dan in the stage version seven years ago when he was a younger man, and now he's absolutely right for Larry' (Foley, see 'Websites' in Further Reading section). Owen had also come to the attention of American audiences in a low budget British film *Croupier* (1998) which had become a surprise hit; from there he built on this reputation in films such as *Gosford Park* (2001) and *The Bourne Identity* (2002).

Natalie Portman was already well known in her own right by the time of *Closer*, with appearances in films such as *Star Wars: Episode II* (2000) and *Cold Mountain* (2002). She had also been directed by Mike Nichols in a 2001 New York theatre production of Chekhov's play *The Seagull*, in which she played Nina. Jude Law had also appeared in *Cold Mountain* with Portman, and come to international prominence in several well received films before *Closer*, including *Wilde* (1997), *AI: Artificial Intelligence* (2001) and *Road to Perdition* (2002).

Before shooting began Nichols spent four weeks working with the four principal actors, which Natalie Portman described as, 'like being in a really interesting English class, analysing the play during rehearsals, bringing in other literary references' (www.sonypictures. com/movies/closer).

Unlike the stage play the film did not use an original score for its incidental music but rather a soundtrack that combined classical and modern compositions that seemed to be chosen in order to complement existing themes. For example, in the scene where Dan first meets Anna at her studio she is playing Puccini's *Madame Butterfly*, an opera about an abandoned woman. Later, when Dan and Anna meet at the opera after Larry has signed divorce papers strains from Mozart's opera *Cosi Fan Tutte* can be heard, a piece of music whose principal theme concerns two couples who swap partners.

The classical music that accompanies much of the film is contrasted with modern songs. Damien Rice's *The Blower's Daughter* begins and ends the film, whereas in the scene where Larry meets Alice in the strip club The Smiths' *How Soon is Now?* is featured, a song whose refrain 'I am human and I need to be loved' seems apt in the respect that both Alice and Larry at this point have been betrayed by their respective partners and temporarily relieve their loneliness through a brief affair after this meeting. However, the latent misogyny of the scene is also highlighted by the Prodigy's *Smack My Bitch Up* which also plays during their encounter in the so-called Paradise Suite.

While critical reaction never reached the superlatives of the stage play, the film version in some respects eclipsed the success of the play. Clive Owen and Natalie Portman where both nominated for Academy Awards and Marber's screenplay was also nominated for a Golden Globe. The film was also immensely successful in financial terms, where the initial production budget of 27 million dollars eventually netted profits worldwide of over 115 million dollars (www.boxofficemojo.com/movies/?id=closer.htm). When one considers the relative lack of action and refusal to produce a 'feel-good' ending, this is something of a real achievement and does much to justify both the complexity and popularity of *Closer*.

4 Workshopping the Play

The exercises and improvisations outlined in this chapter are a series of suggestions for a practical exploration of *Closer*. Formal work through lectures and seminar based discussions can be complemented by testing these ideas out in the rehearsal room. Alternatively they can form the basis for a full-scale production of the play. These suggestions for practical work have come out of my own engagement with the play through classes with students, whereby exercises and improvisations were created in order to engage with some of the themes practically, ideas and problems that the play presents to the actor. The exercises themselves are a combination of existing ideas adapted from the work of other practitioners, but in the main they have been shaped by the very particular demands that *Closer* makes, and were often born out of exigencies that arose from moment to moment in the rehearsal room.

Closer is a challenging play for actors to perform for a number of reasons. The previous chapters have attempted to establish that while the play is concerned with discernable surface appearances, its real themes of human alienation within a modern cityscape are less easy to define or show. Yet, as Richard Eyre observes from Marber's own directing practice in *Closer*, a key to understanding the play must come through a grounding in the following elements of the text: 'meaning, intention, rhythm, nuance, pacing, pausing' (Marber 2004: xi). In this respect *Closer* shares similarities with the work of playwrights such as Samuel Beckett, David Mamet and Harold Pinter, in that when directing their own work, these writers have chosen to reject a neo-Stanislavskian methodology based on ways of establishing character through action: rather they adopt a practice based on producing mood and meaning through verbal patterns and physical rhythms.

On the surface *Closer* seems to be an ideal play on which to base a rehearsal around the precepts of Stanislavskian inspired exercises, whereby nuances of behaviour can be explored through subtext: examples include the incident in scene two in which the actress playing Alice has to communicate that she has secretly overheard Dan saying that he cannot live without Anna (1:2.200–1); also objects such as Dan's sandwich box, or a cashmere sweater can reveal significant truths about a character or situation. Language too, in which surface meaning often conceals more than it reveals, is familiar territory for Stanislavskian based practice. However, as Michael Raab observes, using this method exclusively in rehearsals risks putting undue emphasis on lines such as Alice's, 'I was looking for a cigarette' (1:1.183), whereby instead of becoming, 'just a simple statement [risks] becoming more substantial by ominous pauses' (Raab 2002: 142). Richard Eyre also observed Marber's own frustrations during the first rehearsals for *Closer*, whereby the Stanislavskian inspired training that most of the actors had under-gone at drama school produced the wrong effect for the play:

> [Marber is] exacting almost to a fault and is frustrated that the actors are never quite as accurate enough for him. He finds it hard to trust them . . . He can be exasperated when actors seem confused or obstinate, or wilfully head down a blind alley in their attempts to inhabit a character, demonstrating the truism that the only truth about 'The Method' is that there are as many methods as there actors. (Marber 2004 *Closer*: xi)

Obviously, in any given production the degree of realism employed is a matter for the director and the actors, but it is worth realizing that Marber's language is highly stylized, and that much of *Closer*'s success in performance comes from retaining the precision and self-consciousness of the language rather than approaching the text as a 'slice of life': while this strategy might make the play easier to rehearse and perform, ultimately it will rapidly become unchallenging for the actors and risk boring an audience.

One other caveat to make if thinking of adopting an overly realistic/naturalist approach to *Closer* is the need to remember that in certain scenes, such as Dan and Larry's encounter on the internet, the exchanges are primarily aimed to produce – at least initially – an immediate comic effect rather than any secondary important 'truths' about character or underlying themes of the play. It is the *effect* that words produce – their sounds, emphasis and rhythms that produce meaning rather than any understanding of the character's psychology.

Workshop Exercises

(i) Preliminary work on the text

One useful starting point is to give the actors a 'homework' task before meeting up for the first workshop. This might concern the many verbal associations and discrete imagery that Marber provides in each scene. Many of these repeat or are echoed elsewhere in the play. An overview of these patterns provides a useful starting point in coming to the text and will form the basis of practical work that follows. In the period before the first workshop, ask individuals/small groups to work on individual scenes from the play and complete the following lists:

- Images and locations evoked by the characters – what associations/moods are produced?
- Specific objects that are either mentioned or physically represented – again, what associations/moods do these produce?

- Repetitions of words/phrases used by the characters – encourage the individual/group to make initial suggestions about possible significance.

During the class go through each scene, noting down the observations that are made in each scene on a flipchart/blackboard. By the time all of the findings and summaries have been noted, allow the group to view and digest the recurring motifs/patterns that intervene throughout the scenes. This can then inform the next part of the discussion in which these interlinking patterns can be discussed within the context of the whole play. This initial analysis will hopefully reveal the numerous connections and recurrent motifs in the play: it will also demonstrate – even at this early stage – that *Closer* is far more deceptive than simply being a well-worn tale about adultery between two couples.

(ii) The language of the play

The object of the following exercise is to get the workshop participants to appreciate how carefully (not to say artificially) constructed the language of *Closer* is. The tendency, especially if your group of actors is relatively inexperienced, is to ignore the careful stresses and emphases that Marber deliberately places in the text to help the actor quickly discover the mood, rhythm and tempo in any given exchange between the characters. Instead, actors often highlight the comedy or melodramatic climaxes that the language can also afford – and while this might produce an initially pleasing effect it will impoverish any meaningful or exciting emotional engagement – both for the actors in rehearsal and its audiences in performance.

This exercise can be applied to any scene in the play. However, if used early on in the workshops it might perhaps be best to look at the opening scene as a starting point. The first thing to draw the group's attention to is the specific notation Marber uses in the text.

These take the following forms:

(a) *Italics* – this is most common form of emphasis used. For example:

DAN: I noticed your leg was cut
ALICE: Did you notice my *legs*? (1:1.185)

(b) *Underlining* – this is often used to differentiate between italics when a word or phrase is stressed particularly strongly. In the passage below where Dan remembers Postman's Park, the differences between italicization and underlining are used together in the same sentence.

DAN: I <u>do</u> know it. We sat there . . . (my mother's dead) . . . my
            father and I sat there the afternoon she died.
            She died *here*, actually. <u>She </u>was a smoker (1:1.187)

Occasionally, when special emphasis is called for, both italics and underlining are combined:

ALICE: Men want a girl who looks like a boy. They want to
            protect her but she must be a survivor. And she must
            <u>come</u> . . . like a *train* . . . but with <u>*elegance*</u> (1:1.192)

(c) *Capitalization* – used during moments of high emotion. This does not necessarily mean that the actor is required to shout or deliver the line(s) melodramatically, but it is meant to convey a moment of utter conviction. The device is used quite rarely in the play, but when it is used the actors must pay close attention. Its most frequent use takes place in the parallel break-up scene between Dan/Alice and Larry/Anna in scene six:

Dan moves towards Alice

ALICE: DON'T COME NEAR ME (1:6.231) . . .
ANNA: Why is the sex so important?
LARRY: BECAUSE I'M A FUCKING CAVEMAN (1:6.239)

Initial discussions should involve the whole group in reaching a general consensus on what Marber means by each particular notation device alongside the different combinations used in the text. The following exercise can be used to put these observations into practice:

Upon deciding the particular scene you are going to examine, divide the text up chronologically between the group based on the number of characters in any one given exchange, so that something like a page of dialogue is performed by the actors. Get each group to read aloud the passage amongst themselves. However, when an italicized/underlined/capitalized word or line presents itself the actor should exaggerate it. The form of exaggeration can be decided by the group, but must take the form of a verbal or physical gesture – or both. It may also follow a cue in the text: so for example Alice's line in scene one, 'Do you like it . . . in the dying business' (1:1.184), the emphasis could be given through the sound of a death rattle at the word 'dying'; or it could be physically produced simultaneously with the word being uttered by the actor collapsing to the ground! The aim of the exercise, apart from being fun to perform, is that through exaggeration a sense of the constructed-ness of Marber's language will start to emerge.

After each set of actors has performed their lines in an exagger-ated manner before the whole group, get them to repeat the scene normally, but again asking the actors to pay attention to the areas that Marber has specifically demarcated. Once each group has performed its section in front of everyone, ask them for their comments on what effects were being produced by performing with these verbal stresses.

(iii) Characterization

- **The Obituary Game** – this opening exercise is designed to get your actors to begin thinking about ideas of characterization coming directly from the play itself. In the opening scene Dan tells Alice that in his occupation as a newspaper obituarist euphemisms are employed to both summarize and hint at aspects of the subject not known about in public life, for example: '"He was a convivial fellow", meaning he was an alcoholic' (1:1.188). Alice then asks Dan to apply such a euphemism to his own character ('He was . . . *reserved*') and then herself ('She was *disarming*', 1:1.189).

    Get each person in the group to make a brief summary of the four characters in *Closer* through the same device of euphemisms. The obituary can only be a *maximum* of three sentences long. When reading these out, the workshop leader should assess the differing responses to one specific character in turn. The exercise provides a way of quickly establishing and discussing ideas of characterization, and avoids the clichés of Stanislavskian analysis that actors and students often draw upon in their early engagement with a play text.

- **Alice's car** – throughout the play Alice constructs stories relating to the incident which produced the scar on her leg. Larry believes it to be symptomatic of self-harm; either way, the scar becomes a principal way by which Alice constructs stories about herself and offers a possible clue to the true identity of the real Jane Jones.

    The following improvisation helps to establish both an important aspect of Alice's character – namely her ability to dissemble, which we see in both the opening scene and most obviously at the lap dancing club at the beginning of act two. The following exercise can be applied specifically to the actress playing Alice, or it can be made non-gender specific for a mixed group of people as part of a wider exploration of the play.

The person(s) selected are asked to draw a scar on any part of their body. Before doing so the workshop leader should ask them to think about the following:

– Its size, colour and duration
– Specific properties of the scar – is it numb? does it itch/hurt, etc. ?

Once a few minutes have been taken to think about these various factors, the person draws their scar. Encourage as much detail in the actual drawing as possible – and where realism is not called for, adding small touches such as demarcation of the scar in different colours will be useful in the improvisation to follow.

Once the scar has been drawn ask the person(s) to construct a story based on its aetiology which they are to recount before the group. After the story has been completed ask the group to come up to the person and examine their scar. Encourage the group to ask questions/touch the site of scar/illicit responses from the actor. Allow a few minutes for this to take place and then put the person(s) who have drawn the scar back into the centre of the group to encourage a close questioning about the circumstances and afterlife of the scar. Encourage the questions to be as wide-ranging and detailed as possible. Allow about ten minutes maximum for questioning to take place and then ask the group for feedback on how convincing the story has been.

The improvisation is a variation on 'hot-seating' where a set of given circumstances about a character's background are produced through group questioning. However, in this exercise the emphasis is less on providing a set of 'given circumstances' for the individual, but more a way of facilitating the actor's imagination in dissembling convincingly before a group of would be interrogators.

(iv) Love and seduction

One of the problems that an overly Stanislavskian approach to *Closer* will quickly reveal is that objectives and motivations are made deliberately unclear. Part of the characters' enigmatic qualities are based around their trait of appropriating identities from both strangers and even each other. Much of this unknowability involves the failure to establish logical reasons for why the characters fall in love or eventually leave each other. Explanations given, such as Dan's reasoning to Alice that he leaves her, 'Because . . . I'm selfish and I think I'll be happier with her' (1:6.232), are of limited use to the actor who wishes to 'inhabit' their role. The critic Aleks Sierz makes a useful point about solving these problems practically when he observes that, 'the irrationality of desire' is the key to understanding characterization, and that 'sexual attraction is as much a mystery [in *Closer*] . . . as it is Jacobean drama' (Sierz 2000:194). By this Sierz seems to be saying that other ways of understanding the forces of human attraction and repulsion that govern the play need to be found during rehearsal rather than reaching them via a process of Stanislavskian analysis. Marber also seems to be concordance with the arbitrary and random motivations of his characters, when for instance Alice proposes that '"I will give all my love to this charming man who cuts off his crusts"' (2:9.267). One way of encouraging such a view of the play to actors, especially those who are more familiar with Stanislavskian based training, is through the following exercise.

Divide the group into pairs, preferably with a male and female in each pairing. Ask each person to give their partner an object they own and with which they closely identify themselves, such as a watch or piece of jewellery. Ask each person in turn to improvise a monologue to the group on why this object was the principal reason by which they fell in love with the other person. While the improvisation is taking place their partner should be at their side throughout as a physical presence during the monologue.

If done well, the exercise reinforces a sense that psychological verisimilitude is of less importance in coming to an understanding of *Closer*, and that emotions such as desire or love are governed by forces that the characters can only barely understand.

(v) 'Exciting the imagination'

The critic David Ian Rabey makes an interesting observation in regard to *Closer* when he says, 'seduction is shown as a game in which players do not disclose themselves, but ignite their fellow players imaginations' (Rabey 2003: 200). Alice is particularly good at doing this, in that she manages to both flirt with and subsequently seduce both Dan and Larry by offering glimpses of a constructed self. Primarily she does this through her occupation as a stripper. For instance, when she discloses this information to Dan in the opening scene she only has to mention the word '*stripping*' before she knows that she has captured Dan's imagination completely: 'Look at your little eyes . . . They're popping out. You're a cartoon' (1:1.191).

For this exercise ask each person in the group to talk about three incidents that took place over the weekend. Two of these incidents should be true and one false. Ask the group after each story has been told which they found most interesting/exciting/beguiling. Ask them to explain the reasons why this was so. In most cases the group will find that it is not so much what the person telling the story has said, but what their own imaginations have 'filled in' and extrapolated.

The exercise is useful in the scenes where Alice in particular is using her personae to seduce or attract (such as 1:1, 1:5, 2:7), but it also hopefully gets away from a performance style whereby the actress playing Alice portrays her as a stereotypical vamp, falling back on a stock number of clichéd techniques. It is worth reading through/performing extracts from these scenes after the initial improvisation and afterwards discussing the way seduction is carried out.

For instance, when we first meet Alice in the opening scene she is flirtatious and seductive in her conversation with Dan. This depiction as temptress is given classical connotations, in a reference to what Christopher Innes calls 'the primal sin in the Garden of Eden' (Innes 2002: 433), when Alice eats Dan's apple which she has stolen from his lunch box. This association between Alice/Eve is repeated in scene six where just before Dan is about to leave we see Alice '*asleep curled up on a small sofa . . . A half-eaten red apple beside her*' (1.6.226), although here it is more reminiscent of the brutal image Larry makes about love and the human heart resembling, 'a fist wrapped in blood' (2.10.272).

It is also important to stress that in working on the text practically, while all the characters attempt to attract and seduce they do so with other motives in mind. Again, Alice is a case in point: as a professional stripper her role is to seduce, yet she tells Larry in scene seven that she wears 'armour' (2.7.244), and we must also be aware that despite the seemingly deliberate cultivation of mystery, when Dan asks outright what she wants from life. Alice's reply is 'to be loved '(1.1.192).

In Stanislavskian practice this would be the likely 'super-objective' that the actress playing Alice would take. However, as hopefully these exercises will help to demonstrate, the chameleon-like qualities of love and desire in *Closer* present an exciting challenge in coming to a performance style that attempts to show all the different surfaces – real and constructed that the characters are constantly attempting to reveal and conceal.

Timeline 1989–99

Politics

1989   Communist regimes toppled by revolutions in Eastern Europe; pro-democracy demonstrations in Tiananmen Square savagely repressed by Chinese authorities; major earthquakes in San Francisco; fatwa declared on Salman Rushdie for his novel *The Satanic Verses*

1990   Reunification of Germany; Boris Yeltsin elected President of Russian Republic; Nelson Mandela freed from jail; Iraq invades Kuwait; poll tax introduced in UK – riot in London; Margaret Thatcher resigns as Prime Minister – replaced by John Major

Culture

Plays: Jim Cartwright, *Bed*; Charlotte Keatley, *My Mother Said I Never Should*; Tom Murphy, *A Whistle in the Dark*. Novels: Martin Amis, *London Fields*; Kazuo Ishiguro, *The Remains of the Day*; Jeanette Winterson, *Sexing the Cherry*. Films: *The Cook, the Thief, his Wife, and her Lover*; *Dead Poets' Society*; *When Harry met Sally*; *Sex, Lies and Videotape*

Plays: Howard Brenton and Tariq Ali, *Moscow Gold*; Caryl Churchill, *Mad Forest*; David Hare, *Racing Demon*; Brian Friel, *Dancing at Lughnasa*. Novels: William Boyd, *Brazzaville Beach*; Beryl Bainbridge, *An Awfully Big Adventure*; Antonia Byatt, *Possession*; Hanif Kureishi, *The Buddha of Suburbia*. Films: *Dances with Wolves*; *Edward Scissorhands*; *Ghost*; *The Krays*; *Goodfellas*; *Henry: Portrait of a Serial Killer*; *Pretty Woman*; *Raise the Red Lantern*; *Wild at Heart*. Television: *Twin Peaks*. Music: *Happy Mondays, Pills Thrills and Bellyaches*

Politics

Culture

1991   Mikhail Gorbachev ousted in communist coup – subsequently resigns; Soviet Union dissolves and replaced by commonwealth of independent states; civil war begins in former Yugoslavia; war against Iraq launched

Term 'new lad' coined by Sean O'Hagan in *Arena* magazine. Plays: Alan Bennett, *The Madness of King George III*; John Osborne, *Déjà Vu.* Television: Alan Bleasdale, *GBH.* Novels: Martin Amis, *Time's Arrow*; Angela Carter, *Wise Children*; Simon Nye, *Men Behaving Badly*; Ben Okri, *The Famished Road.* Poetry: Jackie Kay, *The Adoption Papers.* Films: *Prospero's Books*; *Silence of the Lambs; Terminator II: Judgment Day*; *Thelma & Louise.* Art: Damien Hirst, *The Physical Impossibility of Death in the Mind of Someone Living*

1992   European Community recognizes independence of Croatia and Slovenia; Serbs surround Sarajevo and 'ethnic cleansing' of Bosnian Muslims take place; US troops enter Somalia to secure Mogadishu; single market created in Europe; John Major elected Prime Minister; UK government forced to devalue sterling after 'Black Wednesday'; IRA bomb destroys Baltic Exchange in City of London

Publication of Andrew Morton's *Diana: Her True Story* and Susan Faludi's *Backlash.* Plays: David Mamet *Oleanna.* Novels: Victor Headley, *Yardie*; Nick Hornby, *Fever Pitch*; Michael Ondaatje, *The English Patient*; Will Self, *Cock and Bull.* Films: *Man Bites Dog*; *Reservoir Dogs*; *Orlando*

1993   UK ratification of the Maastricht Treaty; IRA bombings in Warrington and City of London – 'Downing Street Declaration' signed; privatization of British Rail;

Publication of John Gray's *Men are from Mars, Women are from Venus.* Plays: Martin Crimp, *The Treatment*; David Hare, *The Absence of War*; Jonathan Harvey, *Beautiful*

Politics

Culture

murder of black teenager Stephen
Lawrence

Thing; Terry Johnson, *Hysteria*;
Harold Pinter, *Moonlight*; Tom
Stoppard; *Arcadia*. Novels: Roddy
Doyle, *Paddy Clarke Ha Ha Ha*; A. L
Kennedy, *Looking for the Possible
Dance*; Vikram Seth, *A Suitable Boy*;
Irvine Welsh, *Trainspotting*. Films:
Naked; *Shortcuts*; *Schindler's List*
Television: *Cracker* (until 1995); *The
X-Files*

1994   Nelson Mandela becomes
President of South Africa; Yasser
Arafat returns to Palestine after 27
years in exile; Russia signs NATO
peace accord; rival tribal genocide in
Rwanda; Russia invades the break-
away state of Chechnya; ceasefire
agreed in Northern Ireland; John
Major's 'Back to Basics' campaign in
public life; death of Labour opposition leader John Smith – succeeded
by Tony Blair; first women priests
ordained in Church of England

Eva Herzigova becomes the 'face' of
Playtex Wonderbra campaign;
Loaded magazine launched in UK;
introduction of National Lottery in
UK. Plays: Caryl Churchill, *The
Skryker & Thyestes*; David Edgar,
Pentecost; Kevin Elyot, *My Night
with Reg*; Harry Gibson *Trainspotting*
(adaptation); Terry Johnson, *Dead
Funny*; Anthony Neilson, *Penetrator*;
Joe Penhall, *Some Voices*; Philip
Ridley, *Ghost from a Perfect Place*.
Novels: Louis de Bernières, *Captain
Corelli's Mandolin*; Jonathan Coe,
What a Carve up! Television: *Friends*.
Films: *Disclosure*; *Four Weddings and
a Funeral*; *Natural Born Killers*; *Pulp
Fiction*. Music: Oasis, *Definitely
Maybe*; Portishead, *Dummy*

1995   Assassination of Israeli Prime
Minister Yitzhac Rabin; Taliban
fighters besiege Afghanistan capital
Kabul; Serbian forces attack Zagreb

Actor Hugh Grant arrested by Los
Angeles police for lewd behavior
with prostitute Divine Brown;
height of 'Britpop' in the UK – beat

Politics

and commit atrocities in the UN controlled enclave of Srebrenica; NATO bombing of Serbia; Bosnian peace accord signed in Paris; John Major resigns and is re-elected leader of the Conservative Party; Labour opposition leader Tony Blair wins Clause Four debate over party commitment to state ownership; broadcasting ban on the IRA lifted

1996   Charles and Diana agree to divorce. Yasser Arafat becomes first President of the Palestinian Authority; Bill Clinton re-elected US President; US troops enter Bosnia as peace-keeping force; Russia signs peace treaty over Chechnya; 18 tourists killed by Islamic terrorists in Egypt; Taliban capture Kabul; IRA bomb Canary Wharf in London; BSE crisis in UK and EC beef export ban; school shooting massacre in Dunblane, Scotland

1997   Cloning of 'Dolly' the sheep; death of Diana, Princess of Wales in a Paris car crash; British leave Hong Kong; Israel begins withdrawal from Hebron; expulsion of weapons inspectors from Iraq; Los

Culture

groups Blur and Oasis occupy number one and two slots respectively in the hit parade. Plays: Sebastian Barry, *The Steward of Christendom*; Jez Butterworth, *Mojo*; David Hare, *Skylight*; Tracy Letts, *Killer Joe*; Phyllis Nagy, *Disappeared* and *The Strip*. Novels: Martin Amis, *The Information*; Pat Barker, *The Ghost Road*; Nick Hornby; *High Fidelity*; Alan Warner, *Morven Callar*. Television: *Jake's Progress*. Films: *Priest*; *Trainspotting*. Music: Pulp, *Different Class*

Plays: Jim Cartwright, *I Licked a Slag's Deodorant*; Ben Elton, *Popcorn*; Mark Ravenhill, *Shopping and Fucking*; Yasmina Reza, Art; Enda Walsh, *Disco Pigs*. Novels: Graham Swift, *Last Orders*; Helen Fielding, *Bridget Jones's Diary*. Film: *The English Patient*; *Brassed off*; *Secrets and Lies*; *Scream*. Television: *The Girlie Show* (until 1997); Dennis Potter, *Karaoke* and *Cold Lazarus*; *This Life* (until 1997)

Sensation exhibition at the Royal Academy London. Plays: April de Angelis, *Playhouse Creatures*; Caryl Churchill, *Blue Heart*; Martin Crimp, *Attempts on her Life*; David Hare, *Amy's View*; Conor McPher-

Politics

Culture

Angeles riots in response to acquittal of four police officers for assault of Rodney King; Labour government win general election with significant majority; Scottish and Welsh devolution approved by referendum

son, *The Weir*; Mark Ravenhill, *Faust is Dead*; Tom Stoppard, *The Invention of Love*. Films: *The Full Monty*; *Spiceworld: The Movie*. Novels: Jim Crace, *Quarantine*; Ian McEwan, *Enduring Love*; J. K Rowling, *Harry Potter and the Philosopher's Stone*; Arundhati Roy, *The God of Small Things*; Film: *Boogie Nights*; *Nil by Mouth*; *The Ice Storm*; *Titanic*

1998   US embassies in Nairobi and Dar-es-Salaam bombed – Osama bin Laden suspected; Zimbabwe President Robert Mugabe orders confiscation of white-owned farms; President Clinton impeached; Air strikes on Iraq; former Chilean dictator General Pinochet detained in the UK; Good Friday Agreement in Northern Ireland

Geri Halliwell leaves The Spice Girls. Plays: Michael Frayn, *Copenhagen*; David Hare, *The Blue Room*; Rebecca Prichard, *Yard Gal*. Novels: Hanif Kureishi, *Intimacy*; Magnus Mills, *The Restraint of Beasts*; Nick Hornby, *About a Boy*; Poetry: Ted Hughes, *Birthday Letters*. Films: *Lock, Stock and Two Smoking Barrels*; *Saving Private Ryan*; *Shakespeare in Love*; *Velvet Goldmine*. Art: Tracey Emin, *My Bed*. Television: *The Cops*; *Will & Grace*

1999   President Clinton acquitted in impeachment trial; Euro currency launched in eleven countries; NATO bombs Kosovo followed by peace plan and installation of NATO peace-keeping troops; shootings by two former students at Columbine High School, Colorado; Scottish Parliament and Welsh Assembly open

Plays: Peter Barnes, *Dreaming*; Mark Ravenhill, *Some Explicit Polaroids*; Richard Norton-Taylor, *The Colour of Justice*. Novels: J. M. Coetzee, *Disgrace*. Films: *Fight Club*; *The Matrix*. Television: Stephen Poliakoff, *Shooting the Past*; *Gimme, Gimme*; *Queer as Folk*

Further Reading

Primary sources

(The editions of *Closer* up to 2004 are significant as they show the changes Patrick Marber made to the play over a seven-year period.)

Marber, Patrick (1997) *Closer*, London: Methuen.
Marber, Patrick (1999) *Closer*. London: Methuen.
Marber, Patrick (2004) *Plays: 1*. London: Methuen.
Marber, Patrick (2007) *Closer*. (This student edition of the play contains a useful introductory commentary and notes by Daniel Rosenthal.)

Secondary sources

Parts of books

Dromgoole, D. (2000) *The Full Room: An A–Z of Contemporary Playwriting*. London: Methuen, pp.193–6 (short provocative piece which simultaneously praises/criticizes Marber's work).
Innes, C. (2002) *Modern British Drama: The Twentieth Century*. Cambridge: Cambridge University Press, pp. 428–35 (useful analysis of Marber's work up to *Closer*).
Rabey, D. I. (2003) *English Drama Since 1940*. London: Pearson Education, pp.195–201 (perceptive analysis of Marber's work in the 1990s).
Sierz, A. (2001) *In-Yer-Face Theatre: British Drama Today*. London: Faber, pp. 187–95 (first major discussion on *Closer*, including

interview material with Patrick Marber, and actors Liza Walker and Mark Strong; outlines plot and discusses influences, critical reception and staging).

Websites

Anna Friel Homepage. www.annafriel.net (contains a useful digest of reviews from the 1999 Broadway production of *Closer* as well as photographs).

Box Office Mojo. www.boxofficemojo.com

Buse, P. British Arts Council: Contemporary Writers. www.contemporarywriters.com (includes a biography and brief, but insightful analysis of Marber's work).

Closer. www.sonypictures.com/movies/closer/site/ (official website of the film version; contains synopsis, character, production notes and trailer).

Closer. www.wikipedia.org/wiki/Closer (useful site containing details on the film, including cast, synopsis, themes, reception, nominations, details of awards and trivia).

Foley, J. *Indie London.* www.indielondon.co.uk/film/closer_feat.html (interview with Marber about the film version of *Closer*).

Greenberg, S. 'The Kindness of Strangers'. www.ramagazine.org.uk (interview with Marber over his interest in the G. F. Watts Memorial in Postman's Park London and its relationship to *Closer*).

Hennigan, A. Interview: Patrick Marber: *Closer.* www.bbc.co.uk/films/2004/12/23/patrick_marber_closer_interview.shtml (interview with Marber who discusses the film version of *Closer*).

Marber, P. www.bbc.co.uk/films/2004/12/23/patrickmarber_closer_interview.shtml (interview about Marber's work on writing for film; available via Realplayer on computer).

Pride, R. (2004) 'Love in Four Letters (or Five)'. www.moviecitynews.com (interview with both Patrick Marber and Mike Nichols on the film version of *Closer*).

Senior, J. 'Sex, Lies and Cyberspace'. www.newyorkmetro.com (short interview with Marber to coincide with the New York opening of *Closer*).

References

Albasani, S. (1997) 'Complex Mating Dance', *Financial Times*, 28 October.

Aston, E. (2003) *Feminist Views of the English Stage*. Cambridge: Cambridge University Press.

Barker, N. (1995) 'Dealing with Confidence', *Observer Review*, 5 February.

Batty, M. (2001) *Harold Pinter*. Northcote House: Tavistock.

Benedict, D. (1997) 'Casualties of Desire', *Independent*, 31 May.

Billington, M. (1996) *The Life and Work of Harold Pinter*. London: Faber.

Billington, M. (1997) 'The Tangled Web of Jealousy and Desire', *Guardian*, May, p. 31.

Bradwell, M. (ed.) (1997) *The Bush Theatre Book: Frontline Drama 5*. London: Methuen.

Brooke, S. (1997) 'Hometown: Wimbledon', *The Times*, 27 September.

Brown, S. and Trodd, C. (eds) (2004) *Representations of G. F. Watts: Art Making in Victorian Culture*. Aldergate: Ashgate.

Burns, E. (1987) *Restoration Comedy: Crises of Desire and Identity*. Basingstoke: Macmillan.

Buse, P. (2006) *British Council Arts: Contemporary Writers*. www.contemporarywriters.com (includes a biography and brief but insightful analysis of Marber's work).

Caesar, E. (2005) 'My Close call with Hollywood', *Independent Review*, 12 January. (Marber talks in some detail about the genesis of *Closer* and its transition to a film version.)

Canfield, J. D. (2001) 'Restoration Comedy', in S. J. Owen (ed.) *A Companion to Restoration Drama*. Oxford: Oxford University Press.

Cavendish, D. (2001) 'And an Enlightening Intellectual Exercise', *Daily Telegraph*, 9 May.

Chambers, C. and Gottlieb, V. (eds) (1999) *Theatre in a Cool Climate*. Oxford: Amber Lane Press.

Chunn, L. and Norman, N. (1998) 'Not in front of your lover', *Evening Standard*, 2 April.

Cooper, T. (1999) 'Anna's Toasting Broadway with Marmite and Teabags', *Daily Mail*, 14 May.

Coveney, M. (1997) 'Double Delight as West End Stages a Revival', *Daily Mail*, 19 December.

Creeber, G. (2004) *Serial Television*. London: BFI.

De Jongh, N. (1998) 'Rejection and Jealousy made Raw and Riveting', *Evening Standard*, 1 April.

Dickson, E. J. (1997) 'Something of the night in him', *Daily Telegraph*, 29 May.

Driscoll, R. (2005) 'Close to the Edge', *The Stage*, 10 February.

Dromgoole, D. (2000) *The Full Room: An A–Z of Contemporary Playwriting* (pp. 93–6). London: Methuen.

Edgar, D. (ed.) (1999) *State of Play*. London: Faber.

Eyres, H. (1998) 'Sensation Stalks the Stage', *The Spectator*, 9 May.

Forrest, E. (1997) 'Patrick Marber: The Upper Hand', *Guardian*, 1 December.

Fray, P. (2003) 'Angry Young Man No More', *The Age*, 17 July.

Gardner, L. (1998) 'Sex in a Chilling Climate', *Guardian*, 3 January.

Garner, L. (1998) 'Closer to the truth?' *Sunday Times*, 19 July.

Gould, V. F. (2004) *G. F. Watts: The Last Great Victorian*. London: Yale University Press.

Greene, S. (1998) 'Enter Genius, from Left', *Independent on Sunday*, 15 March.

Grimley, T. (2001) 'Marber's Keys to Success', *Birmingham Post*, 20 September.

Hanks, R. (1997) 'What's the Deal, Patrick?', *Independent on Sunday*, 11 May.

Innes, C. (2002) *Modern British Drama: The Twentieth Century* (pp. 428–35). Cambridge: Cambridge University Press.

Jenkins, A. (1998) 'The Human Condition: Women can behave badly too', *Independent on Sunday*, 19 July.

Johnstone, S. (1998) 'Press Play for the Cybersex Scene', *The Times*, 18 March.

Kellaway, K. (1998) 'The Secret of *Closer*', *New Statesman*, 1 May.

Kingston, J. (1997) 'Some Kind of Loving', *The Times*, 31 May.

Lyons, D. (1999) '"Closer" Encounters', *New York Post*, 26 March.

Macaulay, A. (1999) 'Magician Casts his Disturbing Spell', *Financial Times*, 22 March.

McRae, J. and Carter, R. (2004) *Routledge Guide to Modern English Writing*. London: Routledge.

Marber, P. (1997) *Closer*, (1999) *Closer*, (2004) *Plays: 1* and (2007) *Closer* (student edition). Editions of *Closer* (see also 'Primary sources' in Further Reading section).

Marber, P. (1995) Interview with Nicholas Wright, *Platform Papers 8: Playwrights*, Royal National Theatre, 1995.

Marber, P. (1996) 'Dramatic moments', *Guardian*, 14 February.

Marber, P. (1997a) Interview with Richard Eyre, April 1997. Programme for *Closer*, National Theatre, May 1997.

Marber, P. (1997b) 'A Book that Changed Me', *Independent on Sunday*, 19 October.

Marber, P. (1997c) Interview with Emma Freud, in *Theatreland*, London Weekend Television, 30 November 1997.

Marber, P. (1998a) 'On Closer', *Evening Standard Hot Tickets Magazine*, 26 March.

Marber, P. (1998b) Interview with Jack Bradley, Programme for *Closer*, Lyric Theatre, March 1998.

Marber, P. (1998c) Interview with Kate Kellaway, *The Observer*, 14 June.

Marber, P. (2001) Interview with Jack Bradley, April 2001. Programme for *Howard Katz*, Royal National Theatre 2001.

Miller, A. (1998) 'The Lunatic Algebra of Love', *The Times*, 4 April.

Motskin, G. (2004) 'Closer', *Creative Screenwriting*, 11(6), 34– 5.

Müller, K. P. (2002) 'Political Plays in England in the 1990s' in B. Reitz and M. Berninger (eds) *British Drama of the 1990s*. Heidelberg: Universitätsverlag C Winter.

Murray, P. (2005) 'My Favourite Londoner', *Time Out London*, 20–27 July.

Naglazas, M. (2006) 'Melancholic Man', *Metro*, 18 March.

Norman, M. (1998) 'A Genius? Don't bet on it', *Sunday Telegraph*, 29 March.

Owen, M. (1997) 'A Stripping Yarn', *Evening Standard*, 23 May.

Owen, M. (1998) 'She's Ready for her Close-Up . . .', *Evening Standard*, 20 March.

Pride, R. (2004) 'Love in Four Letters (or Five)'. www.moviecitynews.com.

Raab, M. (2002) 'Post-feminist Masculinity and all that shit', in B. Reitz and M. Berninger (eds) *British Drama of the 1990s* (pp. 137–48). Heidelberg: Universitätsverlag.

Rabey, D. I. (2003) *English Drama Since 1940* (pp. 195–201). London: Pearson Education.

Robinson, M. (1999) 'Maid in England: Anglicizing Miss Julie', *TijdSchrift voor Skandinavistiek*, 20(1), 29–34.

Sakellaridou, Elizabeth (2000) 'New Faces for British Political Theatre', *Studies in Theatre and Performance*, 20 (1), 43–51.

Sandhu, S. (2005) 'A Dance to the Music of Sex', *Daily Telegraph*, 14 January.

Saunders, G. (2002) Unpublished public interview with Kate Ashfield. *In-Yer-Face? British Drama in the 1990s*, Conference at the University of the West of England, Bristol, 6–7 September 2002.

Seguin, E. (2004) 'Limelight, Camera, Reaction', *The Times*, 16 December.

Shone, T. (1997) 'Up Close and Personal', *Sunday Times*, 26 October.

Sierz, A. (1998) 'Cool Britannia? "In-Yer-Face" Writing in the British Theatre Today', *New Theatre Quarterly*, 14 (4), 324–33.

Sierz, A. (2001) *In-Yer-Face Theatre: British Drama Today* (pp. 187–95). London: Faber.

Simon, J. (1999) 'Love Bites', *New York Magazine*, 5 April.

Smith, B. (1998) 'Why we Hate Women', *Independent on Sunday*, 12 July.

Smith, S. (2004) 'Coming Attractions', *Newsweek*, 30 August.

Soderbergh, S. (1990) *Sex, Lies, and Videotape*. London: Faber and Faber.

Southwell, T. (1998) *Getting Away with it: the inside Story of Loaded*. London: Edbury Press.

Spencer, C. (1997) 'The Triumph: Stand-up Guy', *Guardian*, 31 May.

Stratton, K. (2003) 'Missbehaviour', *Time Out London*, 19–26 November.

Taylor, P. (1997) Review of *Closer*, *Independent*, 25 October.

Urban, K. (2004) 'Towards a Theory of Cruel Britannia: Coolness, Cruelty and the "Nineties"', *New Theatre Quarterly*, 20(4), 354–72.

Whelehan, I. (2000) *Overloaded: Popular Culture and the Future of Feminism*. London: The Women's Press.

Winer, L. (1999) 'Lies in Fiction can be True', *Newsday*, 5 April.

Zoglin, R. (1999) 'Sex in the Trauma Ward', *The Arts/Theater*, 5 April.

Index